SHEW THYSELF A
MAN

BECOMING A MAN OF GOD

ELDON MARTENS

Striving Together Publications
4020 E. Lancaster Blvd.
Lancaster, CA 93535
800.201.7748

Cover design by Andrew Jones
Layout by Craig Parker
Edited by Joan Parish
Special thanks to our proofreaders

ISBN 978-1-59894-162-3

Printed in the United States of America

DEDICATION

In this, my second book, I have been so blessed to have as
my friend and partner in life, my wonderful wife, Martha.
I thank her for her faithful labors in assisting me in this
project. I thank my five children, Mark, David, Stephen,
Kristi, and Matthew, who have encouraged me in writing
this book by their walk with God. So many pastors and
laymen from across the country have challenged me to write
another book, for which I am thankful.

It is with sincere appreciation that I thank my pastor,
Dr. Paul Chappell, for his interest in this second book and
for Brother Cary Schmidt, for his skill and direction in the
final product.

Table of Contents

FOREWORD

Shortly before David's death, he instructed his son, Solomon, "...be thou strong...and shew thyself a man" (1 Kings 2:2).

For many years, Dr. Eldon Martens mentored young men, encouraging and teaching them to embrace biblical principles of godliness. Little did he know when he began this book that, like David's final comments to his son, this book would be Dr. Martens' last written advice to men. Shortly after completing this manuscript, he suffered a major heart attack and the Lord called him home to Heaven.

Dr. Martens was a man who for many years lived what he wrote about in this book. His life was one of sterling integrity and genuine godliness. He was married for over forty-seven years to his godly wife, Martha, and was deeply committed to his five children and fourteen grandchildren.

For over forty years, Dr. Martens served the Lord in full-time ministry, pastoring for many of those years. He pastored

Central Baptist Church in Clovis, California, and he founded the Fundamental Baptist Church in Escondido, California. He pastored these churches for fourteen years each, leading both of them in great spiritual and numeric growth.

In 1992, Dr. Martens stepped out of the pastorate after completely losing his voice from Spastic Dysphonia. During this difficult time, he faithfully served the Lord and never stopped trusting Him. Churches around the nation were thrilled when God restored his voice, even after medical experts said it was impossible.

In 1997, Dr. Martens began a Men's Conference called the "Master's Men." This ministry has touched the lives of hundreds of men and has strengthened and encouraged scores of pastors and local independent Baptist churches.

Dr. Martens' life was marked by a commitment to fundamentalism, including a willingness to practice ecclesiastical separation and, when necessary, to refrain from those who employed or endorsed false doctrine. And yet, he practiced all of that with a gracious, loving spirit and a genuine walk of godliness.

Dr. Martens was a friend to hundreds of pastors and laymen, encouraging and loving them. He was a faithful friend to me for more than a quarter of a century, and I miss him deeply.

In the introduction to this book, Dr. Martens speaks of those who invested in his life, influencing him to live for the Lord as a man of God. For many of us, Dr. Martens would be on a similar list as one who has had a profound influence in our lives. I'm thankful for this, his final challenge and instruction to each of us: "shew thyself a man."

Dr. Paul Chappell
March 2011

INTRODUCTION

Growing up in the small town of Dallas, Oregon, I was greatly influenced by several special men in my life. It began just a couple of days after my birth when my parents invited our pastor over to our home where they prayed over me and dedicated me to be a servant of our Lord. Over the course of my young formative years, my dad, Abe Martens, had a gentle and strong spirit and reminded me that I had been dedicated to the Lord. These qualities helped me to be ever mindful of my accountability to God. I remember my father's prayers at the dinner table as he would pray, often with tears, for my four younger brothers and me. I was blessed to have a good and godly dad to influence my life for God.

Another important figure was my grandfather, Jacob Martens, whose sober admonitions often reminded me to walk with the Lord. I remember that my Saturday responsibility was to mow my grandpa's lawn. When I finished, he provided a small, tasty lunch and then spoke to me about my relationship with the Lord. He often told me how he and some of his family members had fled from Western Russia in 1898 because they had endured religious persecution. He told me accounts of family members being killed before his eyes for their faith in Christ. His godly example and ongoing words of encouragement are still with me to this day. But it was my Uncle John Kliewer, a missionary to Germany, who took a strong interest in me, and when I was an eight-year-old lad, he led me to Christ. There have been a number of other godly men who have played a role in helping to fashion and influence my life.

I believe that each of the faithful mentors God gave me in my life would have all had the desire to say "shew thyself a man." I am reminded of David in the Bible, who truly was a man after God's own heart. When he was at the end of his life, he called his son Solomon to his side and laid a charge upon his heart and life. First Kings 2:1–4 says, "Now the days of David drew nigh that he should die; and he charged Solomon his son, saying, I go the way of all the earth: be thou strong therefore, and shew thyself a man; And keep the charge of the LORD thy God, to walk in his ways, to keep his statutes, and his commandments, and his judgments, and his testimonies, as it is written in the law of Moses, that thou mayest prosper in all that thou doest, and whithersoever thou turnest thyself: That the LORD may continue his word which he spake concerning me, saying, If thy children take heed to their way, to walk before me in truth with all their heart and with all their soul, there shall not fail thee (said he) a man on the throne of Israel."

David's plea to his son was to "shew thyself a man," and even though David struggled and sometimes failed, he remained a man who had a genuine heart for God. David's intimate walk with his God is clearly seen over and over again as we read the psalms. He expresses great hunger in his relationship with his Lord. Psalm 63:1–8 says, "O GOD, thou art my God; early will I seek thee: my soul thirsteth for thee, my flesh longeth for thee in a dry and thirsty land, where no water is; To see thy power and thy glory, so as I have seen thee in the sanctuary. Because thy lovingkindness is better than life, my lips shall praise thee. Thus will I bless thee while I live: I will lift up my hands in thy name. My soul shall be satisfied as with marrow and fatness; and my mouth shall praise thee with joyful lips: When I remember thee upon my bed, and meditate on thee in the night watches. Because thou hast been my help, therefore in the shadow of thy wings will I rejoice. My soul followeth hard after thee: thy right hand upholdeth me."

The great need of this hour is for each one of us men to "shew thyself a man" in our spheres of influence upon the lives of those watching and following us.

Every man has the great potential to be a man of God, regardless of his past failures or present circumstances. I have reflected on the scores of men in the Scriptures who truly became men of God by developing a real relationship with the living God: men such as Enoch, Abraham, David, John the Baptist, and the Apostle Paul. Scores of other little-known men in the Bible likewise became real men of God because they also followed the true and living God. Even today, there are men who exhibit a great testimony as they walk among us.

Either you are already becoming a man of God, or you are a prime candidate to become a man of God. God is not looking for sinless perfection but for men who have a hunger to grow in their walk and to become more like our blessed Saviour. Will you be the man of God that is greatly needed in your home, in your local church, and in a darkened and godless society?

The chapters in this book are a simple but direct tool that could change your life for now and for eternity. Will you pursue the path that will follow after David's challenge to his son Solomon to "shew thyself a man" and become the man of God the Lord desires you to be?

God bless you in your journey through this book.

Dr. Eldon Martens

PART ONE

The Foundation of Becoming a Man of God

Before the structure of a building can go up there must first be a solid foundation, and this foundation is Christ and our relationship with Him.

CHAPTER ONE

The Man's Will

The mind is the citadel of a man's life, and from this
powerful engine our wills determine where we are driven.

B y nature we are at odds with our Creator, even as Adam proved, and we are prone to rebel against a loving God. The only road to becoming a man of God is the path of the surrendered will from which we can make right choices. Even decisions that seem small and unimportant will impact our lives. Going a certain route to our job may keep us from getting bogged down in traffic or maybe avoid a traffic accident down the road; however, every decision we make affects our lives spiritually.

The Bible is filled with challenges to God's people to choose wisely. For example, Joshua called out to the people of Israel in Joshua 24:14–16, "Now therefore fear the LORD, and serve him in sincerity and in truth: and put away the gods which your fathers served on the other side of the flood, and in Egypt; and serve ye the LORD. And if it seem evil unto you to serve the LORD, choose you this day whom ye will serve; whether the gods which your fathers served that were on the other side of the flood, or the gods of the

Amorites, in whose land ye dwell: but as for me and my house, we will serve the LORD. And the people answered and said, God forbid that we should forsake the LORD, to serve other gods."

We find Elijah on Mount Carmel crying out to God's people in 1 Kings 18:21: "And Elijah came unto all the people, and said, How long halt ye between two opinions? If the LORD be God, follow him: but if Baal, then follow him. And the people answered him not a word."

Calls to make spiritual choices were made to individuals as well as groups. For instance, the Lord challenged Peter and Andrew in Matthew 4:18–20: "And Jesus, walking by the sea of Galilee, saw two brethren, Simon called Peter, and Andrew his brother, casting a net into the sea: for they were fishers. And he saith unto them, Follow me, and I will make you fishers of men. And they straightway left their nets, and followed him."

Many other illustrations could be presented here, but in each case people were faced with the grave responsibility to choose. Right choices are not always easy or immediately profitable. However, every wise decision reaps blessings and benefits from a sovereign, omnipotent God.

As I look back through my past, there have been minor and major choices that caused me to move ahead or to get mired down and go backward. I remember when the Lord called me to surrender my life to His will to go into the ministry. I was a recent college graduate with a lucrative teaching position in one of the most desirable school districts and geographic locations in the United States. I loved my teaching positions in the high school and nearby state college.

On that Sunday night in November of 1966, through the faithful preaching of my pastor, I had to choose to either follow my plans or to follow God's will for my life. It was a major choice because I already had a wife and son. Many well-intending friends and relatives suggested that we just stay right where we were and serve the Lord in our comfort zone. When we loaded up all of our worldly possessions in that old Dodge van and headed off for Bible college, we had no job and no place to live. We had only the assurance that our decision was God's will for our lives. I cannot imagine where I would be today had I not surrendered my will to my loving Lord. The path the Lord calls you to may not be easy, but down the road you will look back and say, "I'm so glad I chose this path."

The story is told of a missionary society that contacted the missionary David Livingstone, who was serving in the heart of Africa. They wrote, "Dear Dr. Livingstone, Have you found a good road to where you are? If so, then we want to know how to send other men to join you." Dr. Livingstone replied, "If you have men who will come only if they know there is a good and easy road to follow, I don't want them. I want men who will come even if there is no road at all."

It seems we often choose the road that looks good and is easy for us to tread. The Lord calls, and sometimes His directions are diametrically opposed to our plans. Today the Christian ranks of men are often filled with weak-willed men who faint and fail to follow the Lord's directions. Men are needed who will blaze a trail while following our Guide.

Ezekiel sent out this most profound call to those of his day who had turned away from the Lord when he said in Ezekiel 22:30: "And I sought for a man among them, that should make up the hedge, and stand in the gap before me for the land that I should not destroy it; but I found none." What a tragic statement that with so many who could have stepped up to stand in the gap and make up the hedge, most people were not willing to make the choice that would have spared the nation of Israel from God's judgment.

Our choice must be to follow the directives of God so that our lives and those for whom we are accountable might be spared from certain disaster. With today's hectic schedules and the many directions our lives are being pulled, we must be willing to choose the Lord's path.

David on his deathbed addressed his son Solomon yearning for Solomon to follow his commitment to the Lord. Here are some steps to follow if you and I are going to show ourselves as men of God.

A Decision to Follow Christ

Notice 1 Kings 2:1–2: "Now the days of David drew nigh that he should die; and he charged Solomon his son, saying, I go the way of all the earth: be thou strong therefore, and shew thyself a man."

Be ready.

"…I go the way of all the earth…"—v. 2A

Solomon was reminded of the certainty of death. No one is exempt as we know our lives could end at any moment. James 4:13–15, "Go to now, ye that say, To day or to morrow we will go into such a city, and continue there a year, and buy and sell, and get gain: whereas ye know not what shall be on the morrow. For what is your life? It is even a vapour, that appeareth for a little time, and then vanisheth away. For that ye ought to say, If the Lord will, we shall live, and do this, or that."

We must not assume we will live long lives, but be ready to meet our Maker at any moment. According to Hebrews 9:27: "And as it is appointed unto men once to die, but after this the judgment." If you were to stand before the living God in the next few moments, would you be ready?

The greatest tragedy is when men who knew about Christ were never truly saved the Bible way. Jesus made this sad statement in Matthew 7:21–23: "Not every one that saith unto me, Lord, Lord, shall enter into the kingdom of heaven; but he that doeth the will of my Father which is in heaven. Many will say to me in that day, Lord, Lord, have we not prophesied in thy name? and in thy name have cast out devils? and in thy name done many wonderful works? And then will I profess unto them, I never knew you: depart from me, ye that work iniquity."

Are you absolutely sure you are ready if death were to come today? Being prepared for eternity is more than having good religion, giving to a Christian cause, serving in some capacity, or doing meritorious works. There is nothing you can do to be sure you are going to Heaven except to understand your helpless, hopeless condition as a Hell-bound sinner. Romans 3:23 states: "For all have sinned, and come short of the glory of God." Then by a decision of the mind and heart, you must turn to Christ Jesus who paid for your sins in full, trust in Christ, and receive Him as your personal Saviour. The Bible says, "But as many as received him, to them gave he power to become the sons of God, even to them that believe on his name:" (John 1:12). The Apostle Paul said it well in Acts 20:21: "Testifying both to the Jews, and also to the Greeks, repentance toward God, and faith toward our Lord Jesus Christ."

If there is any doubt regarding your eternal destiny, look to Christ right now and pray this simple prayer with real faith (Remember, it's not the words but the attitude of the prayer that brings salvation)—"Dear God, I come to You right now as a helpless, Hell-bound sinner, recognizing my hopeless condition, and I ask for Your full forgiveness. Lord Jesus, I am right now trusting in Your sacrifice for me on the Cross, as You shed Your blood and paid for my sins and rose again from the dead. I now receive You as my personal Saviour. Thank You for saving me today. Amen." Don't put this decision off as Paul admonishes in 2 Corinthians 6:2: "…behold, now is the accepted time; behold, now is the day of salvation."

Men who are born again must be willing to follow Christ and submit their wills to walk in obedience before Him.

Be strong.

"...be thou strong..."—v. 2B

Many men will choose to devote themselves to some physical routine or body building program. But the strength a Christian needs is spiritual—from the Lord. A man may be physically strong but spiritually frail. We are challenged to be strong spiritually. Ephesians 6:10 says, "Finally, my brethren, be strong in the Lord, and in the power of his might." Second Timothy 2:1 states, "Thou therefore, my son, be strong in the grace that is in Christ Jesus."

Then Paul compares developing physical strength to pursuing spiritual strength in 1 Timothy 4:8. "For bodily exercise profiteth little [for a little time]: but godliness is profitable unto all things, having promise of the life that now is, and of that which is to come." Choose to pursue spiritual strength as you exercise yourself in prayer, Bible reading, study, and daily godly living.

Be a man.

"...shew thyself a man."—v. 2C

Today's society views real men as aggressive and muscular in appearance and macho in disposition. But God sees real men quite differently. Micah 6:8 says, "He hath shewed thee, O man, what is good; and what doth the LORD require of thee, but to do justly, and to love mercy, and to walk humbly with thy God?" Godly Christian men need God's strength of character and a humble spirit so that the world can see that they are different from it.

A Dedication to God's Word

"And keep the charge of the LORD thy God, to walk in his ways, to keep his statutes, and his commandments, and his judgments, and his testimonies, as it is written in the law of Moses, that thou

mayest prosper in all that thou doest, and whithersoever thou turnest thyself."—1 Kings 2:3

Keep the charge.

"And keep the charge of the Lord thy God…"—v. 3a

Solomon is to obey the charge by doing all that God has commanded. Any man who has served in our country's military service knows full well that when a command is given, the immediate response is to be, "Yes, Sir" or "Aye, Aye, Sir." Why is it then that so many men who would immediately obey the command of an earthly authority, would disobey the command of our heavenly authority? We must obey promptly. First Samuel 3:10 says, "And the Lord came, and stood, and called as at other times, Samuel, Samuel. Then Samuel answered, Speak; for thy servant heareth." The Lord calls us to follow Him in obedience, but do we listen and obey as Samuel did?

Walk in His ways.

"…to walk in his ways…"—v. 3b

It has often been rightfully said that "the will of God will not lead you where the grace of God cannot keep you." We often fear that following God's way will lead to something we will not enjoy or something we cannot handle. But the God who directs you in His way knows all about you and will only lead you in ways that are for your eventual good. Being obedient brings us to comprehend that truth and does not lead us to "dead end paths."

Keep His Word.

"…to keep his statutes, and his commandments, and his judgments, and his testimonies, as it is written in the law of Moses…"—v. 3c

You may say that trying to obey all these is very difficult, yet Jesus Christ reminds us in Matthew 11:28–30, "Come unto me, all ye that labour and are heavy laden, and I will give you rest. Take my yoke upon you, and learn of me; for I am meek and lowly in heart: and ye shall find rest unto your souls. For my yoke is easy, and my burden is light."

When we yield our will to Him, keeping His Word becomes our joy. Obedience brings peace. Psalm 119:165 says, "Great peace have they which love thy law: and nothing shall offend them."

Experience the results.

"…that thou mayest prosper in all that thou doest, and whithersoever thou turnest thyself:"—v. 3D

Blessing can only follow when we make choices that submit to the Lord's authority. The word *success* is only found in the Bible once—in Joshua 1:8: "This book of the law shall not depart out of thy mouth; but thou shalt meditate therein day and night, that thou mayest observe to do according to all that is written therein: for then thou shalt make thy way prosperous, and then thou shalt have good success." No matter where we look for blessing and success, we will find them only by following God's Word.

A Devotion to a Godly Legacy

What will you leave behind when you leave this world? Many men leave a substantial amount of material wealth but leave no great spiritual legacy. Solomon's spiritual legacy depended on his following the Word of God. What will you leave behind to your family and others you have influenced?

David established a great legacy for Solomon to inherit. He transferred the leadership of a nation from the house of Saul and established the royal house of David. One day its majesty will be seen when Jesus Christ, the Son of David, sits on His throne to rule the entire earth.

David's greatest legacy is found in Acts 13:22, "And when he had removed him, he raised up unto them David to be their king; to whom also he gave testimony, and said, I have found David the son of Jesse, a man after mine own heart, which shall fulfill all my will." It is God's judgment that he was a man after His own heart.

The choices we make in life and the decisions we follow come from our own will. Will you show yourself a man who is following after the living God?

SUMMARY OF THIS CHAPTER

I.   A Decision to Follow Christ
II. A Dedication to God's Word
III. A Devotion to a Godly Legacy

ACTION STEPS

Here are some action steps you can take to put into practice following God's will. (Initial and date when completed.)

1. Think of one small decision in your daily walk where you have failed to follow Christ. Write that step out on a 3x5 card and commit to follow Christ in this area.

   Initial _____ Date _____

2. Write out Psalm 119:9–11 on a 3x5 card and put it to memory.

   Initial _____ Date _____

3. List what three key areas of a godly legacy you wish to leave behind. Write them out and put them inside your Bible.

   Initial _____ Date _____

CHAPTER TWO

The Man's Walk

God is much more interested in your relationship with
Him than He is in your service for Him.

After we choose to walk with the Lord, our lives will show the quality of the relationship. If our walk is not right, then our lives will be much different from what we expected.

I heard the story of a young man who loved marshmallows more than anything in the world. He ate marshmallows all day long. He even had marshmallow topping on all of his food—for breakfast, lunch, and dinner. One night he had a dream that he was given two giant marshmallows to eat. They were huge! Yet he did all he could to stuff them into his mouth. In the morning when he awoke from his wonderful dream he discovered that both of the pillows on his bed were gone. His dream became his nightmare!

Don't wake up one day, after dreaming of great blessings for your life, only to realize you are living a nightmare. Galatians 6:7–9 says, "Be not deceived; God is not mocked: for whatsoever a man soweth, that shall he also reap. For he that soweth to his flesh shall of the flesh reap corruption; but he that soweth to the Spirit shall of the Spirit reap life everlasting. And let us not be weary in well doing: for in due season we shall reap, if we faint not." Some men delight to sow their wild oats and then pray for a crop failure. But the law of the harvest cannot be altered even as Job 4:8 states, "Even as I have seen, they that plow iniquity, and sow wickedness, reap the same."

Conversely, sowing the right seed in the right way brings the right and desired results. Hosea 10:12 says, "Sow to yourselves in righteousness, reap in mercy; break up your fallow ground: for it is time to seek the LORD, till he come and rain righteousness upon you." The amount that we sow will bring proportionate results. Second Corinthians 9:6 states, "But this I say, He which soweth sparingly shall reap also sparingly; and he which soweth bountifully shall reap also bountifully."

The Lord wants us to spend time with Him in fellowship as we develop as believers. Two themes from Scripture that can enrich us are first, God walked with man before the Fall, and second, fallen, sinful man can now walk with God.

From the very beginning "the Lord God formed man of the dust of the ground and breathed into his nostrils the breath of life; and man became a living soul" (Genesis 2:7). God walked with Adam in the cool of the morning and evening time until sin entered into the picture and ruined that sweet fellowship. Since then, the living God has continued to walk with us because we were created for fellowship with Him. Even when sin had broken that fellowship, God made a way to restore us through a blood sacrifice, a picture of the final sacrifice made on Mount Calvary.

Christ left His heavenly realm descending to this sin-cursed world to deliver us and to restore our fellowship with Him. The eternal, holy, spotless Son of God came to be born of a virgin in a stable. He lived, walked, and suffered as no man ever suffered, eventually going to the Cross to pay for our sin. Now by His sacrifice, fellowship is restored to those who come to Christ and receive Him as their Saviour.

The second great theme is the amazing fact that fallen, sinful men can now walk with their Creator, the living God. This message permeates all of Scripture. Men from all strata of life are afforded this marvelous privilege. This invitation extends to you regardless of where you have been or what you have done. The great delight of our God is to enjoy fellowship with each of us. But, although there are millions of born-again believers, seemingly few diligently pursue this path of intimate fellowship with God.

The phrase, "walking with God" is not just some poetic language. Walking with God can be a powerful experience that will bring great fulfillment to your life.

God has always called men to walk with Him. The Lord wants you to be that man. Second Chronicles 16:9 begins, "For the eyes of the Lord run to and fro throughout the whole earth, to shew himself strong in the behalf of them whose heart is perfect toward him…." The rest of that verse tragically states, "…Herein thou hast done foolishly: therefore from henceforth thou shalt have wars." The reason for our conflicts and turmoil is that we do not walk with God and allow Him to rule in our lives.

Abraham accepted God's invitation to walk with Him. Called out of his native land to a place he had never seen, he set out across the heated desert to walk with God. Moses, by faith, walked with God in obedience. Hebrews 11:27 says, "…for he endured, as seeing him who is invisible." Joshua and Caleb, who despite the great opposition they faced, determined to walk with God.

Enoch stands out as one who "walked with God," living out his name, "dedicated." Genesis 5:21–24 says, "And Enoch lived sixty and five years, and begat Methuselah: And Enoch walked with God after he begat Methuselah three hundred years, and begat sons and daughters: And all the days of Enoch were three hundred sixty and five years: And Enoch walked with God: and he was not; for

God took him." For three hundred years after his son was born, he faithfully walked with God.

I have often thought of that statement and thought of my own brief time on this earth, saved now for almost sixty-one years. I must confess that my journey as a child of God has not always been consistent. In November of 1966, I surrendered my life to the Lord, and so my walk has only been forty-three years, so brief in comparison with that of Enoch. The walk Enoch had with his Lord was extraordinary as we note in verse 24 "And Enoch walked with God: and he was not; for God took him." Something unique was going on in the walk that Enoch had with his Creator because God just took him home—apparently not by death as He does us.

There can be no greater experience in life than to walk with God. When God incarnate walked this earth many years ago, He called men to follow and walk with Him. At first, more than eighty responded. Of these, eventually only twelve remained, and one of those betrayed him. I believe one of the most tragic statements in the Bible is found in John 6:66, "From that time many of his disciples went back, and walked no more with him." Here were disciples who were followers of the Master, yet they left Him.

Maybe you have, for whatever reason, stopped following the Lord. Nevertheless, He is waiting to welcome you back as you seek His forgiveness because you desire to walk with Him once again.

What does it mean to walk with God in a real relationship?

Walking with God Requires Agreement

The Bible clearly states in Amos 3:3, "Can two walk together, except they be agreed?" There must be a oneness of mind if we want to walk with God intimately. We must be on the "same page" with God. We can all have our opinions, but ultimately, the Lord and His Word must be our final authority. Paul said it well in Romans 3:4, "God forbid: yea, let God be true, but every man a liar...."

We need to learn to love what God loves and to hate what God hates. Above all, we must have a love for God's Word as the psalmist expressed continually in Psalm 119 where all 176 verses speak of the Word. Diligently read and study God's precious Word, and you will find yourself more and more in agreement with the Lord.

Walking with God Requires Faithfulness

We have already seen in the life of Enoch a faithful walk for three hundred years (Genesis 5:22). Enoch had a unique relationship with God, and year after year, these two walked together.

There is something to be said for couples who can testify of many years of marriage together. The length of any relationship expresses a real measure of commitment because times of challenge cause some measure of separation. If we find ourselves separated from God, guess who has moved? We are the unstable ones finding ourselves drawn away by our lusts and enticed. Do not allow people, things, or circumstances to draw you away; rather, keep a consistent walk with God.

We are running a race that is not a sprint, but a marathon; do not faint along the way, but run with patience. Hebrews 12:1 says, "Wherefore seeing we also are compassed about with so great a cloud of witnesses, let us lay aside every weight, and the sin which doth so easily beset us, and let us run with patience the race that is set before us." The word *patience* literally speaks of endurance, or "keeping on keeping on," laying aside weights and sins that hinder us. Some men are like fireworks; they begin with a great burst of enthusiasm but quickly fizzle out. Keep your walk faithful; you are in the race for the long haul.

Walking with God Requires Fellowship

Walking with Christ requires interaction with Him as we share our hearts together. Hebrews 11:6 states, "But without faith it is impossible to please him: for he that cometh to God must believe that he is, and that he is a rewarder of them that diligently seek him."

We have been saved by the grace of God and by faith in Christ. We must develop an obedient walk of faith because 2 Corinthians 5:7 says, "For we walk by faith, not by sight." The Lord is delighted when we walk with Him in simple faith, sharing all our desires, needs, and goals with the one who always waits to hear from us.

It was said of Moses that he was a friend of God, and that God spoke to him as a friend. Exodus 33:11 says, "And the LORD spoke unto Moses face to face, as a man speaketh unto his friend...." This relationship of openness between the two provides real fellowship because there is communication both ways. Psalm 25:14 says, "The secret of the LORD is with them that fear him; and he will shew them his covenant." The Lord wants to communicate with us, to reveal the secrets of His heart to us. Talk with your friend, the Lord, throughout the day and develop that connection of fellowship.

Walking with God Requires Separation

The concept of biblical separation is repulsive to some, but without this principle operating in our lives, we will not enjoy a deep, meaningful walk with God. The Scriptures state clearly in 2 Corinthians 6:16–18: "And what agreement hath the temple of God with idols? for ye are the temple of the living God; as God hath said, I will dwell in them, and walk in them; and I will be their God, and they shall be my people. Wherefore come out from among them, and be ye separate, saith the Lord, and touch not the unclean thing; and I will receive you, And will be a Father unto you, and ye shall be my sons and daughters, saith the Lord Almighty."

Jesus called Peter, James, and John to leave their familiar nets, boats, and friends to follow the Master. Jesus calls us, as well, to leave behind those old attitudes, habits, practices, and friends to walk a fresh walk with Him. We now have a new life, a new Master, and a new walk. We are challenged to "walk in newness of life."

As Paul says in Ephesians 4:22–24, "That ye put off concerning the former conversation the old man, which is corrupt according to the deceitful lusts; And be renewed in the spirit of your mind; And that ye put on the new man, which after God is created in righteousness and true holiness." Our goal must be to get as close to our Lord in our daily walk as we can by avoiding those things that would take us away from Him.

Walking with God Requires Confidence

As we learn to walk with God, a greater measure of confidence comes in our walk with Him. Over time, trials give opportunity for the Saviour to show Himself real on our behalf. David enjoyed that confidence as stated in Psalm 23:4, "Yea, though I walk through the valley of the shadow of death, I will fear no evil: for thou art with me; thy rod and thy staff they comfort me."

Even in the dark valleys of despair and seeming hopelessness, we can have confidence in the one who stated in Matthew 28:20, "...and, lo, I am with you alway, even unto the end of the world. Amen." (I love that "Amen" which emphasizes, "so be it.") Hebrews 13:5 states, "...for he hath said, I will never leave thee, nor forsake thee."

The longer we walk with the Lord, the more our confidence grows because, according to Hebrews 7:25, "Wherefore he is able also to save them to the uttermost that come unto God by him, seeing he ever liveth to make intercession for them." The longer the walk, the greater our confidence.

Walking with God Requires Progress

The ultimate goal of a consistent walk with God is progress in our lives. The Lord spoke to Joshua (Joshua 1:2–3), "Moses my servant is dead; now therefore arise, go over this Jordan, thou, and all this people, unto the land which I do give to them, even to the children of Israel. Every place that the sole of your foot shall tread upon, that have I given unto you, as I said unto Moses."

As Joshua and the people obeyed their God, doors opened; they made progress; they found themselves going to places that they never dreamed were possible. God wants us to step out, to go places, and to progress in life. Allow the Lord to lead you to new heights of victory, new dimensions of faith, and new service for His glory.

A real walk with God is available to each of us. Our God wants that intimate walk even more than we do. Begin today to move towards a deeper, closer walk with your Saviour.

SUMMARY OF THIS CHAPTER

This chapter shows us that God wants to work with us and that we can walk with Him.

    I.   Walking with God Requires Agreement
   II.   Walking with God Requires Faithfulness
 III.   Walking with God Requires Fellowship
 IV.   Walking with God Requires Separation
  V.   Walking with God Requires Confidence
 VI.   Walking with God Requires Progress

ACTION STEPS

Here are some action steps you can take to move forward in your walk with God. (Initial and date when completed.)

1.   List several steps you need to take in developing a genuine walk with God. Write them out on a 3x5 card, and keep it in your Bible.

    Initial _____ Date _____

2.   Read the testimony of Enoch as he walked with God, and memorize Genesis 5:22 and 24.

    Initial _____ Date _____

3.   Think of what most hinders your walk with God, and confess that area to the Lord, asking Him to give you the victory you need.

    Initial _____ Date _____

CHAPTER THREE

The Man's Worship

Worship is not an activity, but an attitude
coming from a surrendered life.

This third basic quality of a man seeking to become a man of God is his desire to worship God. Real worship is the overflow of a surrendered, committed walk with God that will be expressed through our actions and our adoration of our Lord.

Today so much emphasis is made in evangelical and charismatic movements on a particular form of worship. I am afraid that even with all the sincere efforts to worship the living God, the heart of our loving Father is greatly grieved by the empty efforts of so many professing believers. Much outward "worship"—uplifted hands, dance, and even tears—miss the Lord's view of worship. Many sincere people try to worship someone or something, but the real God is overlooked.

When the word *worship* is used, we believing Christians immediately think of some mystical experience or remember a trip to nature to view the handiwork of the Creator. But worship must be part of our daily walk with God. So many times we feel that we must be in a specific place, singing a special hymn, or finding ourselves overcome by an emotional experience to be truly worshipping God. The Word of God is filled with many accounts of those who worshipped the Lord.

The wise men came from afar and finally saw the Saviour. Matthew 2:11 says, "And when they were come into the house, they saw the young child with Mary his mother, and fell down, and worshipped him: and when they had opened their treasures, they presented unto him gifts; gold, and frankincense, and myrrh." When we truly see our Saviour, we will also worship Him.

King Jehoshaphat and the people of Judah were threatened by three invading armies. Afraid, Jehoshaphat prayed, and the Lord answered in 2 Chronicles 20:15: "…Thus saith the LORD unto you, Be not afraid nor dismayed by reason of this great multitude; for the battle is not yours, but God's." And in response "…Jehoshaphat bowed his head with his face to the ground: and all Judah and the inhabitants of Jerusalem fell before the LORD, worshipping the LORD" (2 Chronicles 20:18).

In a few moments of time, Job lost all he had—his possessions, family, and health. Yet the Bible says that Job "…fell down upon the ground, and worshipped" (Job 1:20). Even in despair and tragedy, a believer can truly worship.

One day when we get to Heaven, worship will be an eternal activity of every child of God. According to Revelation 4:10–11: "The four and twenty elders fall down before him that sat on the throne, and worship him that liveth for ever and ever, and cast their crowns before the throne, saying, Thou art worthy, O Lord, to receive glory and honour and power: for thou hast created all things, and for thy pleasure they are and were created."

Worship happened and will happen at different times in a variety of circumstances using all kinds of people. What does worship mean? The word *worship* comes from an old English word that expresses honor, worth, or worthiness. The Hebrew word in the Old Testament means to pay homage and bow down in adoration. The New Testament Greek word means to show reverence, respect or to serve as a minister. Therefore, real, biblical worship involves our attitudes, actions and our adoration.

Why do we not truly worship as we should?

The Problems of Worship

When Paul was in Athens, on Mars' hill, he found many people worshipping, and they even had an altar erected to worship "the unknown god." They were so fearful they might overlook some deity that this special altar was built in case they had missed some god.

Many people fail to worship God because they do not know Him through faith in His Son, Jesus Christ.

Unbelief is a great hindrance to those who desire to worship. We must believe in the one we desire to worship and not just go through the motions without real faith in Him.

Unconfessed sin is a great deterrent to worshipping the Lord because it hinders communication with God. Fellowship with God is essential to worship, and sin prevents it because we become cold and insensitive to our Lord.

Wrong attitudes can also cause a lack of real worship. Anger or bitterness will cause God to ignore our "worship" until we get things right with others. In chapter 5:22–23, Matthew writes that we need to seek forgiveness before coming to worship the Lord.

The Person We Worship

It is said that man was made to worship; therefore, he cannot help worshipping. But who or what will he worship? Here are some vital ingredients needed to rightly worship God.

Whom to worship

Our worship is right only when we worship God as He is described in His Word. Many have a distorted, inadequate view of God and do not understand who God is or what His attributes are. You cannot rightly worship someone you do not know.

In 1 Chronicles 16:7–36, David praises God. In verse 29 he says "Give unto the Lord the glory due unto his name: bring an offering, and come before him: worship the LORD in the beauty of holiness." Here are fifteen attributes of God so we can better know whom we worship.

1. He is a person—He is not some force or mystical being. Our Lord possesses all the qualities of personality with intelligence, emotions and will. He is immeasurably greater than we are. He can relate to us, but we can relate to Him only through His Son.

2. He is eternal—He is from everlasting to everlasting. He has no beginning and no end; we cannot understand eternity.

3. He is a Spirit—John 4:24: "God is a spirit: and they that worship him must worship him in spirit and in truth."

4. He is omniscient—Our God is all knowing, unlimited in His vast knowledge and understanding. We cannot conceal or hide anything from the Lord.

5. He is omnipotent—The omnipotence of God means that He can do anything He chooses to do.

6. He is omnipresent—He is always present everywhere.

7. He is sovereign—Regardless of turmoil, confusion, or chaos everywhere, God does all things according to His purpose. He has no "Plan B."

8. He is unchangeable—God is not fickle, but unchanging in character and purpose; yet He is always loving, true, and powerful. "Jesus Christ the same yesterday, to day, and for ever" (Hebrews 13:8).

9. He is good—God is always good in character, "…no good thing will he withhold from them that walk uprightly" (Psalm 84:11).

10. He is righteous and just—He always deals fairly with all His creation.

11. He is truthful—Everything He says is true, and everything He does is truthful.

12. He is holy—He is completely free of any moral defect, compromise or contamination. He is the standard of excellence that we cannot (in this life) reach.

13. He is creator—In the beginning God created the universe *ex nihilo* (i.e., out of nothing).

14. He is sustainer—He alone holds all things together or the universe would come apart (Colossians 1:17).

15. He is judge—He is the fully righteous and fair judge before whom the entire human race will stand someday.

Why we should worship

God created within each one of us the need to worship. We were made for worship, and we will never be fulfilled until we worship the Creator who made and redeemed us. His great desire is to receive from us true worship that glorifies Him.

We also are *commanded* in the Scripture to worship. Mark 12:28–30 says, "And one of the scribes came, and having heard them reasoning together, and perceiving that he had answered them well, asked him, Which is the first commandment of all? And Jesus answered him, The first of all the commandments is, Hear, O Israel; The Lord our God is one Lord: And thou shalt love the Lord thy God with all thy heart, and with all thy soul, and with all thy mind, and with all thy strength: this is the first commandment." We are to love and reverence the Lord with every part of our lives. He is worthy of all our worship.

The Procedure of Worship

According to Revelation 4:10–11: "The four and twenty elders fall down before him that sat on the throne, and worship him that liveth for ever and ever, and cast their crowns before the throne, saying, Thou art worthy, O Lord, to receive glory and honour and power: for thou hast created all things, and for thy pleasure they are and were created."

Here we find a great picture of how to truly worship the Lord. The event described in this passage will take place in Heaven just after the Rapture. Here the twenty-four elders engage in great triumph and praise as they worship the Lamb of God. Look at what they do and say:

They fall down.

Worship begins with a right attitude. "…four and twenty elders fall down before him…" (v. 10). Psalm 95:6 says, "O come, let us worship and bow down: let us kneel before the LORD our maker." Even the devil understands worship as he tempted the Lord Jesus, challenging the Saviour to worship him: Matthew 4:8–9, "Again, the devil taketh him up into an exceeding high mountain, and sheweth him all the kingdoms of the world, and the glory of them; And saith unto him, All these things will I give thee, if thou wilt fall down and worship me."

Worship cannot take place unless we are willing to humble ourselves. Five times in the New Testament the Lord tells us to humble ourselves. Notice Peter's words in 1 Peter 5:6, "Humble yourselves therefore under the mighty hand of God, that he may exalt you in due time." Then James 4:6, 10 says, "But he giveth more grace. Wherefore he saith, God resisteth the proud, but giveth grace unto the humble. Humble yourselves in the sight of the Lord, and he shall lift you up."

We must be willing to surrender our rights because we are His possession. Everything we possess is His as well; therefore, giving to the Lord with a cheerful spirit is true worship. We must be willing to be controlled by our Master, but we naturally tend to be proud. God's "hate list" given in Proverbs 6:16–19 begins with "A proud look…." As pride enters, we feel that "no one is going to tell me what to do."

Kneeling certainly goes against the grain in the minds of many, and so an old-fashioned altar call often reveals the haughty spirit of the many men not willing to go forward at the invitation, kneel, and get right with God. Humbling ourselves and falling down shows us God's greatness and our smallness.

They cast crowns.

"…and cast their crowns before the throne" (v. 10). We also worship by right actions. The Bible speaks of at least five specific crowns, listed at the end of this book. A crown can represent anything that exalts the "wearer," or that draws attention to the "wearer." Your crown could be your physique, your possessions, your job, or your position in life.

To Abraham the crown of his life was the arrival of his long promised son. The Lord then called to Abraham in Genesis 22 and told him to sacrifice his beloved son upon an altar, and Abraham immediately obeyed. There, at the base of the mount where he was to sacrifice Isaac, he spoke to his servants: Genesis 22:5, "And Abraham said unto his young men, Abide ye here with the ass; and I and the lad will go yonder and worship, and come again to you." What a powerful testimony of true worship!

All true worship involves some measure of sacrifice. Whether time, goals, a job, or possessions, just give it to Jesus. Remember, "the Lord giveth and the Lord taketh away." Tell the Lord, "You can take it away or You can let me keep it, as You choose." No one who truly worships the Lord wants to be exalted himself; rather, he joyfully lays down his crowns at Jesus' feet.

They acknowledge His throne.

According to Revelation 4:11: "Thou art worthy, O Lord, to receive glory and honour and power: for thou hast created all things, and for thy pleasure they are and were created."

Revelation 5:11–13 again expresses true worship. Men seek to have glory, honor, and power. The results are war, division, strife, divorce, and conflict. When God receives glory, honor, and power, the results are unity, peace, and harmony. He alone is worthy of our praise and worship. From our true worship all our Christian service flows: prayer, giving, soulwinning, teaching, and edifying, among other things. Worship is the great overflow of a surrendered will and a committed walk with our Master.

Worship Him throughout today as your cup gets filled and overflows because you cannot help but lift your heart, hands, and voice in praise and worship.

SUMMARY OF THIS CHAPTER

This chapter gives us a biblical perspective of real worship to our Master.

   I.   The Problems of Worship
  II.   The Person We Worship
 III.   The Procedure of Worship

ACTION STEPS

Here are three action steps you can take to move you closer to a life of true worship. (Initial and date when completed.)

1. Think of three things that have hindered you from worshipping the Lord. Write them out, and commit to seeing those barriers removed.

   Initial _____ Date _____

2. Write out and memorize John 4:24 and Psalm 29:2.

   Initial _____ Date _____

3. List some ways you can worship the Lord this coming week. Again write these out and commit to follow through.

   Initial _____ Date _____

PART TWO

The Structure in Becoming a Man of God

Once a solid foundation is established, then we have something to build upon that will make a difference in every sphere of our lives and in the lives of those around us.

CHAPTER FOUR

The Man's Work

*God must first do a work in us before He
can effectively do a work through us.*

I f any man will be all that God desires him to be, he must have
that genuine relationship covered in the first three chapters. If
we have a beautiful, new, fully loaded car with all the bells and
whistles but it never leaves the garage, it is obviously useless. Just
as a car was designed to be driven and the horse was born to run,
so the Christian man was created to do good works. Ephesians 2:10
states: "For we are his workmanship, created in Christ Jesus unto
good works, which God hath before ordained that we should walk
in them."

Good works begin on the inside, and work their way out. Saved
men who enjoy a real relationship with Christ will want to serve the
Lord and bring glory to His name. The Lord wants to work with us
to produce these good works and glorify Himself in them. We must
willingly allow our Lord to empower us to accomplish His goals
for our lives as in Philippians 2:12–16, which says, "Wherefore, my
beloved, as ye have always obeyed, not as in my presence only, but

now much more in my absence, work out your own salvation with fear and trembling. For it is God which worketh in you both to will and to do of his good pleasure. Do all things without murmurings and disputings: That ye may be blameless and harmless, the sons of God, without rebuke, in the midst of a crooked and perverse nation, among whom ye shine as lights in the world; Holding forth the word of life; that I may rejoice in the day of Christ, that I have not run in vain, neither laboured in vain."

We are to display the Word of Life by our walk, and shine as lights in a crooked and perverse generation. Any man who has no desire to serve our Lord either has a major spiritual issue or has no concept of the Christian life.

Every man, at the moment of salvation, receives at least one spiritual gift to be used to serve in his local church. You might review the chapter on the Holy Spirit in my book, *Steps of a Good Man*, and prayerfully consider areas of ministry in which you have strengths.

Jesus went about doing good. Notice what He said in Matthew 20:26–28, "But it shall not be so among you: but whosoever will be great among you, let him be your minister; And whosoever will be chief among you, let him be your servant: Even as the Son of man came not to be ministered unto, but to minister, and to give his life a ransom for many." If we are to be what God saved us to be, we must serve others because God did not save us to sit, but to serve Him by ministering to others.

There are many valuable lessons to be learned from nature. For example, the honeybee is one of God's smaller creatures, but the average worker bee has the strength to carry its own weight. God will also give us strength to do whatever tasks He gives us.

The bee shows real effort as it flies as far as three miles in search of nectar to make honey. Similarly, any real work for the Lord requires effort. In 1 Thessalonians 1:3 Paul speaks of these believers' "work of faith, and labor of love, and patience of hope."

The word *work* speaks of the task they were engaged in, and the word *labor* means to toil to exhaustion. *Patience of hope* deals with perseverance or staying with the work, looking forward to what God will accomplish.

It is estimated that one pound of honey represents nearly 300,000 miles in "bee flight." I become tired just thinking about that much work! The honeybee seldom dies of old age, but literally works itself to death. To be "busy as a bee" really means having no idle moments because bees are continually engaged in their labor.

Notice what Paul wrote in 1 Corinthians 15:58, "Therefore, my beloved brethren, be ye stedfast, unmoveable, always abounding in the work of the Lord, forasmuch as ye know that your labour is not in vain in the Lord." Solomon stated in Ecclesiastes 9:10, "Whatsoever thy hand findeth to do, do it with thy might; for there is no work, nor device, nor knowledge, nor wisdom, in the grave, whither thou goest."

As many as 50,000 bees labor and live harmoniously together in one beehive for the common good of the colony. As we work and serve our Lord alongside fellow believers, let us always keep in mind the necessity of working in harmony together.

Paul challenged the believers in Philippians 1:27, "Only let your conversation be as it becometh the gospel of Christ: that whether I come and see you, or else be absent, I may hear of your affairs, that ye stand fast in one spirit, with one mind striving together for the faith of the gospel." The Lord is always pleased to find us laboring, living together as Psalm 133:1 states: "Behold, how good and how pleasant it is for brethren to dwell together in unity!"

Unfortunately, some men are lazy and will work hard to get out of work. I heard the story of a man who went to the doctor for a physical exam, stating he was always tired. He said, "Now Doc, tell me in plain language, what's the real problem with me?" The doctor then asked, "Do you really want it straight?" The man said, "Yes, just tell me exactly what the trouble is." "Well," said the doctor, "There is absolutely nothing wrong with you except you are just plain lazy." The patient drawled, "Ok, Doc, now give me the medical term for my problem so I can tell my wife."

God lays a premium on laboring and hard work all throughout Scripture. For example, Proverbs 6:6 says, "Go to the ant, thou sluggard; consider her ways, and be wise."

The parable in Matthew 20:1–16 says:

> For the kingdom of heaven is like unto a man that is an householder, which went out early in the morning to hire labourers into his vineyard. And when he had agreed with the labourers for a penny a day, he sent them into his vineyard. And he went out about the third hour, and saw others standing idle in the marketplace, And said unto them; Go ye also into the vineyard, and whatsoever is right I will give you. And they went their way. Again he went out about the sixth and ninth hour, and did likewise. And about the eleventh hour he went out, and found others standing idle, and saith unto them, Why stand ye here all the day idle? They say unto him, Because no man hath hired us. He saith unto them, Go ye also into the vineyard; and whatsoever is right, that shall ye receive. So when even was come, the lord of the vineyard saith unto his steward, Call the labourers, and give them their hire, beginning from the last unto the first. And when they came that were hired about the eleventh hour, they received every man a penny. But when the first came, they supposed that they should have received more; and they likewise received every man a penny. And when they had received it, they murmured against the goodman of the house, Saying, These last have wrought but one hour, and thou hast made them equal unto us, which have borne the

burden and heat of the day. But he answered one of them, and said, Friend, I do thee no wrong: didst not thou agree with me for a penny? Take that thine is, and go thy way: I will give unto this last, even as unto thee. Is it not lawful for me to do what I will with mine own? Is thine eye evil, because I am good? So the last shall be first, and the first last: for many be called, but few chosen.

Jesus gives this parable in response to Peter's question in chapter 19:27: "Then answered Peter and said unto him, Behold, we have forsaken all, and followed thee; what shall we have therefore?" A parable is an earthly story with a heavenly meaning, and here the Lord deals with working and rewards. The householder is our Heavenly Father. The laborers are followers of the Lord. The vineyard is God's chosen field or the place He has called us to serve Him, and His steward is the Lord Jesus Christ. There are three kinds of workers in the Father's vineyard.

Laborers of the Harvest

Responding workers (vv. 1–2)

They are up early, roll up their sleeves, and go to work while most still sleep. I remember in my first pastorate that there was a section of my town where migrant workers arrived before the sun was up, and at the crack of dawn they anxiously awaited farmers to come by and pick up men to go into the harvest. Romans 13:11 states: "And that, knowing the time, that now it is high time to awake out of sleep: for now is our salvation nearer than when we believed." We need to wake up and get busy serving our Lord, for "the night cometh, when no man can work."

I thank God that during my years as a pastor I had many good, willing men who served the Lord together. I would say from the pulpit that I needed a man to help here or do this, and hands would shoot up saying, "Preacher, use me." The heart of our Heavenly Father is pleased to see men who respond with a heart to serve, saying, "I'll go, I'll serve, you can count on me."

Reluctant workers (vv. 3–6c)

When the householder came later there were men standing around idle in the marketplace. While others worked, these were lazy and apathetic to the great need before them.

The householder came by at the third hour (around 9 AM), then the sixth hour (around noon), and then again at the ninth hour (about 3 PM), and even at the eleventh hour (5 PM) just before the day was done. He said, "Hey men, I've got work for you. There are great opportunities right now, just get on board and let's go to work." Notice how these responded in v. 4b, "…And they went their way." Thank goodness they were finally available to work. Yet as the day had gone on, opportunities to labor were missed.

Often men are preoccupied with their own agenda and personal vineyard. Some men are caught up in their chosen occupation and pursuing a vicious, materialistic circle trying to heap to themselves this world's goods and pleasure. "My house is full, but my fields are empty, who will go and work for me today?" states that familiar song of challenge. I trust you are not one of these reluctant workers, for the Master has need of you today.

Resentful workers (vv. 7–12)

This last testimony is an example that many times men will demonstrate if their motive in serving is not right. The householder agreed to pay these workers a common, fair wage for a day's work, a "penny" (a quarter-size silver denarius worth about 15 ½ cents).

In verse 7 the householder stated, "…whatsoever is right, that shall ye receive." Keep in mind that our Heavenly Father is just and always gives what is right. When paid, the laborers hired early in the morning began to murmur and whine because those who worked fewer hours received the same pay as they did. "It isn't fair because I have worked longer and harder in the heat of the day, and I deserve better compensation than what you are giving me."

Sometimes those who are laboring in the Lord's harvest complain and criticize other workers. The complainers feel undervalued. Maybe the pastor mentioned some other worker and publicly commended the person, and we feel slighted. "Pastor should acknowledge me and give me some public attention, for I deserve this" is what we are thinking. Or, "My name was left out of the bulletin, and I had more on my bus route than that other worker whose name was listed." Let me ask you this question: Why are you serving, and whom are you laboring for? Is it for self-glory, adulation and recognition, or is it for your Master?

Hurt feelings or complaints invariably reveal our wrong motives for serving. Let's be responsive workers, ready to serve our Lord, and not reluctant or resentful in the Householder's vineyard.

Lord of the Harvest

Remember that Jesus is Lord of the harvest, and that He will be fair in rewarding His servant.

He is calling.

The Householder calls for men to labor for Him. A very tragic statement is found in Ezekiel 22:30: "And I sought for a man among them, that should make up the hedge, and stand in the gap before me for the land, that I should not destroy it: but I found none." The Lord looks continually for laborers. Matthew 9:37–38 states: "Then saith he unto his disciples, The harvest truly is plenteous, but the labourers are few; Pray ye therefore the Lord of the harvest, that he will send forth labourers into his harvest."

The householder went looking at every possible time, starting early in the morning, then at about 9 AM, noon, 3 PM and even just before quitting time at 5 PM. The close of the day in first century Judea was 6 PM, and so up to just an hour before the end of the day the master called looking for workers.

Today, men are needed to serve. "Who will work for me today?" He calls out to you reading this chapter. Maybe you are serving now, but what more could you do to bring in the harvest?

He is concerned (v. 1).

This is "his vineyard" (v. 1), and the Master wants to bring in the ripe harvest. Harvest lasts only so long, and then it is too late. Whatever work needs to be done must be accomplished *now*. In John 9:4, Jesus states: "I must work the works of him that sent me, while it is day: the night cometh, when no man can work."

Time is running out, and the crop will be lost. All around us precious souls are perishing, going into a Christless eternity. Put in the sickle now, and do not delay. Jesus said in John 4:35: "Say not ye, There are yet four months, and then cometh harvest? behold, I say unto you, Lift up your eyes, and look on the fields; for they are white already to harvest," (i.e., really ripe). We are losing the harvest because as Jesus said, "the fields are white already to harvest." The crop is almost gone; it is almost too late. So go now; put your hand to the plow; do what you can while you are yet able to serve.

He is coming (v. 8a).

It is almost suppertime as the day has just about ended. All the workers will be gathered in, our toils and labors ended: "So when even was come, the lord of the vineyard saith unto his steward, Call the labourers, and give them their hire, beginning from the last unto the first."

I do not know when the Lord of the harvest will tell His steward, the Lord Jesus, to call His workers home, but His coming is imminent. It could be today. Revelation 4:1, "After this I looked, and, behold, a door was opened in heaven: and the first voice which I heard was as it were of a trumpet talking with me; which said, Come up hither, and I will shew thee things which must be hereafter." Harvest time will be over, suppertime will soon begin, and we will be gathered up to Heaven.

First Thessalonians 4:16–17 says, "For the Lord himself shall descend from heaven with a shout, with the voice of the archangel, and with the trump of God: and the dead in Christ shall rise first: Then we which are alive and remain shall be caught up together with them in the clouds, to meet the Lord in the air: and so shall we ever be with the Lord."

He is consistent (v. 8b).

Once all the workers are gathered home, and the harvest has ended, the Steward will rightly give out the rewards coming to the laborers as He will give them their hire. Second Corinthians 5:10 says, "For we must all appear before the judgment seat of Christ; that every one may receive the things done in his body, according to that he hath done, whether it be good or bad." Revelation 22:12 states, "And, behold, I come quickly; and my reward is with me, to give every man according as his work shall be."

I'm so glad we have a steward that is fair and just to each of us. Matthew 20:15 states: "Is it not lawful for me to do what I will with mine own?" Jesus Christ, the steward, the righteous judge gives according to His perfect character and sovereign judgment: "So the last shall be first and the first last…" (v. 16).

What crown and rewards will you have in that day? What are you doing to serve the Lord in His vineyard? What is the attitude of your heart? He knows perfectly and sees perfectly, and His reward will be consistent. Don't try to figure it all out. Just do your ministry for the Lord and for His glory. Your work will be to your own good.

SUMMARY OF THIS CHAPTER

This chapter deals with our faithful labors for the Master with right motives and attitudes.

    I. Laborers of the Harvest
        A. Responding workers
        B. Reluctant workers
        C. Resentful workers
   II. Lord of the Harvest
        A. He is calling.
        B. He is concerned.
        C. He is coming.
        D. He is consistent.

ACTION STEPS

Here are three action steps you can take to fulfill your duty as a laborer in the Master's harvest. (Initial and date when completed.)

1. List where you have served and where you are serving now, and then compare to see if you are doing more or less for the Master.

   Initial _____ Date _____

2. Get together with your pastor and ask him if you are helping him enough with your labors in the church, and then ask if there is anything else you can do to serve and help.

   Initial _____ Date _____

3. Make a point to pray specifically for a willing spirit and have a readiness to minister when a need arises or when the Holy Spirit prompts you.

   Initial _____ Date _____

CHAPTER FIVE

The Man's Warfare

A man's mind is a strategic citadel and a valued trophy
over which a fierce battle is constantly being waged.

W hen any man receives Christ as Saviour, the battle lines are drawn, and major conflicts begin. When any man surrenders his will, determining to walk with God by worshipping and serving Him, the enemy will try to defeat him. These battles have hurt warriors not prepared for the fight. Every Christian man is forced to fight on more than one front, a situation all military commanders seek to avoid. We fight the enemy from within and from without.

Men have always fought. During all of recorded history, over eight thousand peace treaties have been broken. Man's nature is to war no matter what treaty he has made. The Bible reveals that wars began over six thousand years ago after the fall of man, and wars will continue until the coming of the Prince of Peace at the end of the tribulation. The Battle of Armageddon will be fought against the antichrist and his armies, and four hundred million will die in battle as Christ vanquishes His enemies. It will take six months just to bury the dead from that bloody defeat. Only then will real, lasting peace fill the earth as Jesus Christ, the King of kings and Lord of lords, rules with a rod of iron for one thousand years.

All of the battles and wars in history were a direct result of the depravity of mankind. God's creatures rebelled against their Creator. They shook their fists in the face of their God, plunging the human race into its sinful state. Conflicts are part of every man's life; no one is exempt. The battlefield may be within yourself, in the home, the workplace, the neighborhood, or anywhere.

Those without Christ war with God. The Bible declares that they are the enemies of God. Romans 5:10 says, "For if, when we were enemies, we were reconciled to God by the death of his Son, much more, being reconciled, we shall be saved by his life." And Romans 11:28 states, "As concerning the gospel, they are enemies for your sakes...." When a man is born again he then has peace with God. He is no longer His enemy: "Therefore being justified by faith, we have peace with God through our Lord Jesus Christ:" (Romans 5:1).

For the child of God, while there is forgiveness and peace with God, new conflicts will emerge. We are now Satan's enemies. The believer who was once a child of darkness has become a child of light, and so he faces new, powerful enemies: the enemy within (the flesh), the enemy without (the world), and the enemy around (the devil and his host). Paul, at the end of his life, declared in 2 Timothy 4:7, "I have fought a good fight, I have finished my course, I have kept the faith." This raging war will never end until we get to Heaven.

The Enemy Within

You have a traitor in the camp, the *flesh*. When we get saved, the old flesh is not eradicated, so the conflict is now between the "new man" (Christ's new creation) and the "old man" (our flesh).

Galatians 5:16–17 says, "This I say then, Walk in the Spirit, and ye shall not fulfil the lust of the flesh. For the flesh lusteth against the Spirit, and the Spirit against the flesh: and these are contrary the one to the other: so that ye cannot do the things that ye would." And in Ephesians 4:22–24 we read, "That ye put off concerning the former conversation the old man, which is corrupt according to the deceitful lusts; And be renewed in the spirit of your mind; And that ye put on the new man, which after God is created in righteousness and true holiness." Here we see that the flesh opposes the new man and my liberty in Christ, and wants to bring me to sinful living.

The Great Wall of China provided a tremendous defense against its enemies, but one traitor from within could open a gate and cause great defeat. Our one traitor from within, the flesh, can do unthinkable wickedness, bringing defeat to our lives. Satan and his demons will entice us in any way they can through this traitor, our flesh. James 1:14–15 says, "But every man is tempted, when he is drawn away of his own lust, and enticed. Then when lust hath conceived, it bringeth forth sin: and sin, when it is finished, bringeth forth death."

I saw a bumper sticker some time ago that caught my attention as it read, "I can resist anything except temptation." We are exposed to temptation every day of our lives, and we will struggle with it all of our lives. Some have tried to escape from temptation by various means. Simeon Stylites (AD 390–459) lived for the last thirty-six years of his life on a three-foot-wide platform on a pillar sixty feet off the ground. Prior to that, he spent several months buried in the ground up to his neck. He also lived in an enclosed cell for ten years, as well as spending time in different monasteries. His efforts may have reduced the amount of temptation but never eliminated it.

How do we handle these temptations that appeal to our flesh? Consider the Lord Jesus when He was tempted time and time again. Hebrews 4:15 states: "For we have not an high priest which cannot be touched with the feeling of our infirmities; but was in all points tempted like as we are, yet without sin." Beginning His public ministry with baptism in the Jordan River, He faced major temptations in the same basic areas, as we do and Adam did. First John 2:16 says, "For all that is in the world, the lust of the flesh, and the lust of the eyes, and the pride of life, is not of the Father, but is of the world."

Lust of the flesh

Matthew 4:2–4 says, "And when he had fasted forty days and forty nights, he was afterward an hungred. And when the tempter came to him, he said, If thou be the Son of God, command that these stones be made bread. But he answered and said, It is written, Man shall not live by bread alone, but by every word that proceedeth out of the mouth of God."

Jesus, after His forty day fast, was hungry. The temptation appealed to the flesh just as Adam and Eve faced in Genesis 3:6, "...the tree was good for food...." Likewise, our flesh cries out for gratification. We succumb to gluttony, wrong sexual appetites, bodily abuse, just to "feel good," and we pervert the good.

Lust of the eyes

Matthew 4:8–9 says, "Again, the devil taketh him up into an exceeding high mountain, and sheweth him all the kingdoms of the world, and glory of them; And saith unto him, All these things will I give thee, if thou wilt fall down and worship me." The temptation appealed to the eye. Imagine what our Saviour viewed—the lands, cities, vineyards, etc. Genesis 3:6 says that the fruit was "...pleasant to the eyes..." and beautiful to Adam and Eve.

Today we are consumed by what the eye gate sees. Materialism says that we must have all of "this stuff" for ourselves—new cars, new clothes, houses, boats, motor homes, jewelry, rings, etc. All of these "things" consume our lives if we are not careful. There is nothing wrong with the "things" that God provides, as long as He remains preeminent, not them.

Pride of life

Matthew 4:5–6 says, "Then the devil taketh him into the holy city, and setteth him on a pinnacle of the temple, And saith unto him, If thou be the Son of God, cast thyself down: for it is written, He shall give his angels charge concerning thee: and in their hands they shall bear thee up, lest at any time thou dash thy foot against a stone." Our Lord was probably on the southeast corner of the temple facing the Kidron Valley with, no doubt, many people watching from below. The same temptation came to our first parents in Genesis 3:6, "...to be desired to make one wise..."; and in verse 5, they could "...be as gods...."

Often our flesh is tempted by our pride to be angry, jealous, bitter, envious, and covetous. The only remedy to defeat the flesh is to starve and discipline it through the power of God's Word as Jesus did when Satan tempted Him. We must have the power of the Holy Spirit to control us and the church to strengthen us.

The Enemy Without

We are not to be friends with the world's system which is controlled by Satan, called the prince of this world in John 12:31. We are challenged in James 4:4: "Ye adulterers and adulteresses, know ye not that the friendship of the world is enmity with God? whosoever therefore will be a friend of the world is the enemy of God."

Jesus said in John 17:14–16, "I have given them thy word; and the world hath hated them, because they are not of the world, even as I am not of the world. I pray not that thou shouldest take them out of the world, but that thou shouldest keep them from the evil. They are not of the world, even as I am not of the world." We are in the world, but the world is not to be in us. Otherwise, we become worldly, defeated men.

This world is not becoming better, but rather more wicked. Demonic forces control it. Our world system is diametrically opposed to God and what is right. The Bible says in 1 John 5:19, "And we know that we are of God, and the whole world lieth in wickedness." Literally, the whole world is cradled in the arms of the devil. God has kept us in this dark world to be a light, a reflection of His glory by fighting Satan, by proclaiming the Good News, and by godly living. Matthew 5:16 says, "Let your light so shine before men, that they may see your good works, and glorify your Father which is in heaven."

The Enemy Around

We can have victory over the enemy's army even though they seem very strong. First John 4:4 says, "Ye are of God, little children, and have overcome them: because greater is he that is in you, than he that is in the world."

September 11, 2001, was one of the darkest days in America's history. The images of those planes flying directly into the Twin Towers in New York City forever remain in our minds. Those evil, cowardly terrorists, motivated by two objectives—the taking of innocent lives and the destruction of America—were controlled by Osama Bin Laden, the attack's mastermind. Today, terrorist cells lie in wait, ready to act to take away our freedom and destroy us.

The spiritual Osama Bin Laden is Satan, and he is aided by an army of demons. Their objective is to destroy all godly things. Paul tells us as soldiers of the Cross in Ephesians 6:10–13, "Finally, my brethren, be strong in the Lord, and in the power of his might. Put on the whole armour of God, that ye may be able to stand against the wiles of the devil. For we wrestle not against flesh and blood, but against principalities, against powers, against the rulers of the darkness of this world, against spiritual wickedness in high places. Wherefore take unto you the whole armour of God, that ye may be able to withstand in the evil day, and having done all, to stand."

Satan's goal is your defeat and destruction. The Lord warned Peter in Luke 22:31: "And the Lord said, Simon, Simon, behold, Satan hath desired to have you, that he may sift you as wheat." We must note the methods he uses to corrupt us. Second Corinthians 11:3 says: "But I fear, lest by any means, as the serpent beguiled Eve through his subtilty, so your minds should be corrupted from the simplicity that is in Christ."

Men everywhere allow anxieties, fears, doubts, impure thoughts, cares, and incorrect thinking to fill their lives. Satan wants to make inroads into your life through several areas you leave open.

The inroad of unchecked sins

Unconfessed, harbored sin is an inroad which invites the devil: Ephesians 4:27, "Neither give place to the devil." Sin, left unchecked, is like a cancer cell that will begin to spread and grow. It may be unchecked attitudes like anger, bitterness, wrath, or malice; or actions like lying and cheating; or wicked thoughts in our lives that are left alone. The answer is to repent and confess that specific sin. First John 1:9 says: "If we confess our sins, he is faithful and just to forgive us our sins, and to cleanse us from all unrighteousness." In Revelation 2–3, five of the seven churches are called on to repent of their prevailing sins.

The inroad of unguarded thinking

Many men allow their minds to roam freely, leaving their thoughts unguarded. We must guard our minds and keep them from being routed by the enemy. Second Corinthians 10:4–6 says, "(For the weapons of our warfare are not carnal, but mighty through God to the pulling down of strong holds;) Casting down imaginations, and every high thing that exalteth itself against the knowledge of

God, and bringing into captivity every thought to the obedience of Christ; And having in a readiness to revenge all disobedience, when your obedience is fulfilled."

Solomon also gave a warning in Proverbs 4:23: "Keep thy heart with all diligence; for out of it are the issues of life." Your computer, television, magazines, and music allow corrupted ideas to enter your unguarded mind. Any good gardener will keep the weeds of wickedness out of his garden. James 4:7 says, "Submit yourselves therefore to God. Resist the devil, and he will flee from you." Resist and say "NO" to any wicked enemy trying to enter. Also, you are the only one who can resist your flesh, so arm and defend yourself with the sword of the Spirit, the Word of God.

The inroad of unchecked desires

This day of freely used tranquilizers, drugs, and alcohol has brought about many defeats. Scores of God's soldiers have been wounded, some permanently scarred because these unchecked appetites gain entrance into their lives. God the Holy Spirit makes His home in our bodies. First Corinthians 6:19 says, "What? Know ye not that your body is the temple of the Holy Ghost which is in you, which ye have of God, and ye are not your own?"

The answer for unchecked appetites is to let the Holy Spirit renew our minds daily, especially in the areas that have been damaged and need to be refortified as Romans 12:2 tells us, "And be not conformed to this world: but be ye transformed by the renewing of your mind, that ye may prove what is that good, and acceptable, and perfect, will of God."

The inroad of unrelegated concerns

We live in a complex, pressure-filled society, and many men are busy with work, family, finances, and many other activities. It is very easy to get overloaded and pinned down by the enemy. We can find ourselves depressed because of our overwhelming life-styles.

Our lives can seem to be spiraling down with no way out and no visible hope in sight.

The answer is "remembrance" as we need to get our eyes back on the Lord. Hebrews 12:2 says: "Looking unto Jesus the author and finisher of our faith; who for the joy that was set before him endured the cross, despising the shame, and is set down at the right hand of the throne of God."

God's Word is filled with hope and many precious promises. We must "think right" if we want to find ourselves back in our place of duty, marching on. Remember Paul's words in Philippians 4:8: "Finally, brethren, whatsoever things are true, whatsoever things are honest, whatsoever things are just, whatsoever things are pure, whatsoever things are lovely, whatsoever things are of good report; if there be any virtue, and if there be any praise, think on these things."

Remember the words of 1 Peter 5:7: "Casting all your care upon *him*; for *he* careth for you" (emphasis added). So if unrelegated cares and concerns are weighing you down, turn to the one who saved you and loves you, and let Him help carry your burdens.

The famous battle of Waterloo decided the fate of Napoleon and the destiny of Europe. Napoleon made a crucial decision. Throughout the battle Napoleon kept his famous cavalry in reserve. They were the finest soldiers in the world and had never known defeat. Seeing the battle go against him, he at last gave the order for them to charge.

On came this fearless cavalry, galloping full speed toward the British, seemingly invincible. However, there was a sharp dip in the field, a trench that neither Napoleon or his soldiers knew was there and where Wellington had placed his finest sharpshooters. As the thundering horsemen came, unexpected volleys of shots met them. Horses fell; soldiers were hit. The cavalry turned, regrouped and charged again, but the sharpshooters prevailed. The battle of Waterloo was lost. The hidden danger of that dip had brought defeat, a hidden danger that Napoleon never saw. Be careful of the many hidden dangers awaiting you on the battlefield, and be prepared.

Victory is not just possible but certain in our spiritual battles as we avail ourselves of all that our Commander has given us. Every battle begins in our minds, valued trophies over which fierce battles are constantly being waged. Paul likens the mind to a citadel or strategic stronghold, and the enemies within and without will battle to the death to take control. Proverbs 23:7 states: "For as he thinketh in his heart, so is he…." It has been said, "Sow a thought and you reap an act. Sow an act and you reap a habit. Sow a habit and you reap a character. Sow character and you reap a destiny."

The whole process begins in the mind, so follow Peter's admonition in 1 Peter 1:13–16: "Wherefore gird up the loins of your mind, be sober, and hope to the end for the grace that is to be brought unto you at the revelation of Jesus Christ; As obedient children, not fashioning yourselves according to the former lusts in your ignorance: But as he which hath called you is holy, so be ye holy in all manner of conversation; Because it is written, Be ye holy; for I am holy."

SUMMARY OF THIS CHAPTER

This key chapter presents man's enemies in spiritual warfare and the steps that will give him the promised victory.

    I. The Enemy Within—Flesh
        A. Lust of the flesh
        B. Lust of the eyes
        C. Pride of life
    II. The Enemy Without—World
  III. The Enemy Around—Devil
        A. The inroad of unchecked sins
        B. The inroad of unguarded thinking
        C. The inroad of unchecked desires
        D. The inroad of unrelegated concerns

ACTION STEPS

Here are three action steps you can take to fulfill becoming a stronger soldier for Christ. (Initial and date when completed.)

1. Honestly list your specific areas of weakness as you deal with the enemy from within. List these on paper before the Lord, and pray over these.

    Initial _____ Date _____

2. As you face the enemy from without, what can you do to minimize this area of attack in your life? Write down specific steps you will take to avoid temptations.

    Initial _____ Date _____

3. Your formidable enemy is walking about seeking whom he may devour. Resisting him is the key. Write on a 3x5 card and memorize James 4:7–8.

Initial _____ Date _____

CHAPTER SIX

The Man's Weapons

*Any man facing the enemy unprepared—with a lack of
commitment and with improper weapons—is doomed for defeat.*

Our enemies are formidable and relentless in their efforts to bring us down in defeat. The enemy will attack with even greater intensity as time continues and this world becomes more and more opposed to God. To combat the enemy effectively God gives us an arsenal of weaponry to use. We must take careful aim and hit the target, using God's weapons.

I heard the story of a commanding general visiting the troops on the front line during the Korean War. As the general walked along, all of a sudden three sniper bullets came whizzing over his head. Immediately the general barked out to the sergeant at his side, "Where's that sniper?" The sergeant replied, "Sir, we know exactly where the sniper is located." "Well then, take him out—shoot him!" replied the general. The sergeant replied, "Sir, that sniper has been shooting at us for six weeks and hasn't hit anyone yet, and we're afraid if we take him out they will replace him with someone who can shoot straight."

Many warriors are not shooting straight because they are not focused. Maybe they are shooting blanks and are thus ineffective in their efforts to defeat the enemy. Here are some important weapons we must become familiar with and use properly to have victory.

The Weapon of Commitment

No warrior will survive unless he is committed to vanquish the enemy. Christian soldiers walk in defeat, not because of inadequate weapons, but because of inadequate commitment. We must resolve to be conquerors. A half-hearted try will not win the battle. Do not be shaped by your past defeats, but march ahead and take out the enemy. The battlefields are strewn with many who gave up or were sidetracked during the battle. Remember, we are already victors in Christ. Romans 8:37 says: "Nay, in all these things we are more than conquerors through him that loved us." Victory is yours and every man's, if he is serious and committed to win the battle.

The Weapon of Comprehension

The enemy will defeat us if we do not understand him. We must have wisdom. The battlefields of history are strewn with the wreckage of courageous, but ill-prepared, ill-equipped soldiers.

At the famous battle of the Little Big Horn, George Armstrong Custer recklessly pitched his men against a much larger force of Sioux and Cheyenne warriors. In the ensuing battle, his regiment was totally destroyed, and he and all 210 men under his immediate command were killed. In the same way, when the Nazi Blitzkrieg rolled into Poland, a brigade of Polish cavalry gallantly but foolishly charged a formation of German tanks. The troopers' lances and swords were no match for the panzer's cannons and machine guns, and they were all slaughtered.

Our enemies are stronger and wiser than we are, and we must realize that we cannot win using our tactics, our ingenuity, or our strength. Knowing our foe and knowing the futility of relying on our strength are the keys to defeat our enemy. First Corinthians 10:12 says, "Wherefore let him that thinketh he standeth take heed lest he fall."

The Weapon of Confidence

Total confidence in Christ is the most powerful weapon that we have. The Apostle Paul stated in Philippians 4:13: "I can do all things through Christ which strengtheneth me." Second Corinthians 10:3–4 gives several insights, one of which is that our weapons are not earthly, but heavenly, spiritual: "For though we walk in the flesh, we do not war after the flesh: (For the weapons of our warfare are not carnal, but mighty through God to the pulling down of strong holds;)."

David knew when he faced Goliath that victory came only from the Lord. First Samuel 17:46–47 says, "This day will the LORD deliver thee into mine hand; and I will smite thee, and take thine head from thee; and I will give the carcases of the host of the Philistines this day unto the fowls of the air, and to the wild beasts of the earth; that all the earth may know that there is a God in Israel. And all this assembly shall know that the LORD saveth not with sword and spear: for the battle is the LORD's, and he will give you into our hands." Imagine that young lad standing face to face with Goliath and giving him that powerful statement, "…for the battle is the LORD's…."

The Apostle Paul, in 1 Corinthians, reminds us that even though our flesh and human resources limit us, our victory over spiritual enemies comes from the Lord and is spiritual. Paul again addresses this truth in Ephesians 6:12: "For we wrestle not against flesh and blood, but against principalities, against powers, against the rulers of the darkness of this world, against spiritual wickedness in high places." These spiritual weapons are not weak, but they are "mighty" through God even to the taking down of any stronghold.

A *stronghold* is a metaphor for the fortresses that ancient cities had, usually on top of a hill south of the city. This was a strong, fortified, and defensive place where the defenders could hide and fight. Yet we now can face a powerful stronghold and see that stronghold pulled down. No enemy or stronghold can stand against the sheer power of God's arsenal. Do not try to fight a spiritual enemy with a human weapon because you will be doomed to defeat.

The Weapon of Compliance

To be victorious in spiritual warfare, we must bring our minds into compliance with God's truth. Notice what Paul states in 2 Corinthians 10:5, "Casting down imaginations, and every high thing that exalteth itself against the knowledge of God, and bringing into captivity every thought to the obedience of Christ."

Remember, the citadel of a man is his mind, for "out of it are the issues of life" (Proverbs 4:23). Proverbs 23:7a says, "For as he thinketh in his heart, so is he...." We must be careful to keep our minds clear of any sinful attitudes and activities. We must choose to filter out every wrong thought that arises, cast it down, and throw it out.

A sick soldier is ineffective against the enemy. An army overtaken by some influenza or disease is facing a great possibility of defeat. One of the knights of King Arthur's Round Table, Sir Galahad, was often called the Maiden Knight by Tennyson because of his pure life. Tennyson said of Galahad, "His strength was as the strength of ten, because his heart was pure." Christian soldiers fall in battle because the sickness of sin has infected their lives. Sinful thinking will drain you, as David found out when he entertained adultery first in his mind and later in his actions.

Guard your mind, and keep out all thinking that is against the knowledge of God, and bring under the control of God every evil or sinful thought.

The Weapon of Contending

The victorious soldier realizes the critical value of strict discipline to make sure he is a ready contender. Notice 2 Corinthians 10:6, "And having in a readiness to revenge all disobedience, when your obedience is fulfilled." We must be ready to fight any wrong thought to protect our minds. We must be ruthless in disciplining what we allow to occupy our thinking. It has been said, "You can't stop a bird from flying over your head, but you can stop it from building a nest in your hair." Be ready to retaliate against any enemy of the mind.

In John Bunyan's great allegory, *Pilgrim's Progress,* the protagonist, Christian, decides to leave the main highway and follow another path that seems easier. But the path leads him into the territory of Giant Despair who owns Doubting Castle. Eventually he is captured by Giant Despair and kept in a dungeon and advised to kill himself. For the first time it seemed as if Despair had really conquered Christian.

Then Hope, Christian's companion, reminds him of previous victories that he had experienced. And Saturday, at midnight, they began to pray and continued until almost morning. A little before day, Christian, as one half-amazed, broke out in passionate speech and declared, "What a fool am I thus to lie in this stinky dungeon when I may as well be at liberty. I have the Key of Promise that will, I am persuaded, open any lock in Doubting Castle." Then said Hope, his companion, "That's good news, good brother, pluck it out of thy bosom, and try the key." He did, and the prison gates flew open.

Many are in bondage to what I call stinkin' thinkin' and find themselves in despair and doubt. Do not stay there, but "revenge all disobedience" by casting out every wrong thought, replacing it with right thinking. Philippians 4:8 states: "Finally, brethren, whatsoever things are true, whatsoever things are honest, whatsoever things are just, whatsoever things are pure, whatsoever things are lovely, whatsoever things are of good report; if there be any virtue, and if there be any praise, think on these things."

The Weapons of Conquest

No greater soldier exists than the Lord Jesus Christ. His victorious conquests give us the secret of victory as our Saviour vanquished every foe He faced. What weapons and tactics did He use to be victorious? In Matthew 4:1–11, He faced Satan and was tempted by the lust of the flesh, the lust of the eyes, and the pride of life.

We are also tempted in these same three areas. First John 2:15–16 states: "Love not the world, neither the things that are in the world. If any man love the world, the love of the Father is not in him. For all that is in the world, the lust of the flesh, and the lust of the eyes, and the pride of life, is not of the Father, but is of the world." The Lord, in each venue of battle, faced Satan with "It is written" as He quoted the Word of God. The Word is weaponry for the Christian soldier.

Paul, in his letter to the Ephesians, in chapter 6:13–18 says, "Wherefore take unto you the whole armour of God, that ye may be able to withstand in the evil day, and having done all, to stand. Stand therefore, having your loins girt about with truth, and having on the breastplate of righteousness; And your feet shod with the preparation of the gospel of peace; Above all, taking the shield of faith, wherewith ye shall be able to quench all the fiery darts of the wicked. And take the helmet of salvation, and sword of the Spirit, which is the word of God: Praying always with all prayer and supplication in the Spirit, and watching thereunto with all perseverance and supplication for all saints."

No army would go to battle knowing that their weapons were defective or inferior. Every commander wants his troops fitted with the very best weapons possible. Today's military forces are outfitted with the latest and most efficient of weaponry.

During the Revolutionary War, a British regiment was ordered to charge a body of French infantrymen. The trumpets sounded, and the attack began as the British soldiers boldly moved towards the French army. However, as soon as contact was made, the British broke rank like a wave hitting a rock. The retreating British had been sacrificed to a traitor's fraud. Their swords and lances had not been forged out of tempered steel, but out of a worthless and inferior metal. At the first stroke their swords bent and snapped. No matter how brave and determined their hearts, they were no match without the right quality of weapons.

Many men have fallen due to inferior, obsolete weapons. Therefore, we are commanded in Ephesians 6 several times to "put on the whole armour of God" that we might stand against our enemies: "…if God be for us, who can be against us" (Romans 8:31). Each particular piece of armor is forged out of the Word of God. Notice the powerful weapons of conquest that we are to "put on" and take with us (verses 11 and 13).

Knowing the Word

Paul begins with "the belt or girdle of truth," which was vitally necessary for any soldier in Paul's day (Ephesians 6:14a). The Roman soldier always wore a tunic of loose-fitting clothing, and since ancient combat was largely a close contact, hand-to-hand battle, this large leather belt was essential. Wrapped around his loins and waist area, it would firmly tuck in the loose tunic and hold together the rest of his armor.

It is absolutely necessary that we are gird about with the truth of God's Word. If a Christian does not spend time in the truth and know the truth, he will be easy prey for the enemy. The Scriptures declare "Thy Word is truth" (John 17:17, Ephesians 1:13, Colossians 1:5), and the Christian soldier must prepare for each day by reading God's Word as he faces the enemy. Second Timothy 2:15 says: "Study to shew thyself approved unto God, a workman that needeth not to be ashamed, rightly dividing the word of truth." The Bible will be the garment that will enable us to maintain a life of purity. This first piece of armor is key to winning battles.

Obeying the Word

The next weapon, the breastplate of righteousness, is found in verse 14b. A Roman soldier dared not go into battle without his breastplate—a tough, sleeveless piece of armor that covered his full torso. This armor, made of leather, heavy linen or metal, was there to protect the heart, lungs, intestines, and vital organs.

This symbolizes the warrior's righteousness in Christ by putting on the new man as seen in Ephesians 4:24–27: "And that ye put on the new man, which after God is created in righteousness and true holiness. Wherefore putting away lying, speak every man truth with his neighbour: for we are members one of another. Be ye angry, and sin not: let not the sun go down upon your wrath: Neither give place to the devil."

Paul rejoiced in his imputed righteousness which God alone bestows, but Paul realized the necessity of daily walking in newness of life by living righteously as he stated in Romans 6:13, "Neither yield ye your members as instruments of unrighteousness unto sin: but yield yourselves unto God, as those that are alive from the dead, and your members as instruments of righteousness unto God."

So to put on the breastplate of righteousness is to live moment by moment in obedience to God's Holy Word by the power of the Holy Spirit. God supplies the standard by His Word, and He supplies the power by the Holy Spirit.

Giving the Word

Without proper footwear, the soldier is virtually worthless on the battlefield. The Roman soldier wore sandals or sometimes boots with nails or spikes on the sole to give him sure footing. If we are going to "stand" and "withstand," our feet must be firmly fixed with the "preparation of the Gospel of peace" (v. 15). We must first have full assurance that we are saved and have peace with God: Romans 5:1, "Therefore being justified by faith, we have peace with God through our Lord Jesus Christ."

Then we, with beautiful feet, can carry the Good News, the Gospel of peace to the multitudes around who are falling at the hands of the enemy: Romans 10:15, "And how shall they preach, except they be sent? as it is written How beautiful are the feet of them that preach the gospel of peace, and bring glad tidings of good things!" Soldiers of Jesus Christ must be sure-footed and prepared each day to give the Gospel out to others along the way. The most victorious Christian is the soulwinning Christian.

Satan has declared war; as soldiers of the Cross we must bring a message of peace and victory. Romans 5:18 states, "Therefore as by the offence of one judgment came upon all men to condemnation; even so by the righteousness of one the free gift came upon all men unto justification of life." Because you are justified by Christ, stand your ground firmly, and give out the Gospel of peace.

Believing the Word

We are now challenged to add to our armor. In verse 16, "Above all" carries the thought, in addition to all—to all that has preceded, add the shield of faith. Roman soldiers had several kinds of shields that were used in their day. One was a small, round shield about 1½ ft. to 2 ft. in diameter and was secured to the arm by a leather strap.

However, the shield mentioned here is not lightweight but is much larger (2½ ft. wide and about 4½ ft. high) and is designed to protect the entire body of the soldier. Made of a solid piece of wood and covered over with metal or heavily oiled leather, this defensive armor was carried to the front line of battle by soldiers who normally stood side by side forming a huge line extending even a mile long. The enemy would shoot or hurl darts or arrows dipped in some flammable substance and ignite them. The large shield would protect the soldier from these fiery missiles.

When lies, blasphemous thoughts, and wicked imaginations are hurled at us, we have a great weapon, our faith in God's Word. It is our faith in the Word that protects us. According to Proverbs 30:5, "Every word of God is pure: he is a shield unto them that put their trust in him." How big is your shield?

Receiving the Word

The fifth piece of armor is found in verse 17a, and is the helmet without which no Roman soldier entered into battle. Some of the helmets were made of thick leather, covered with metal plates. Others were heavy molded or beaten metal and usually had cheek pieces to protect the face. The purpose, of course, was to protect the head from injury, particularly from the broad sword. That weapon was a large two-handed, double-edged sword about three to four feet long.

Notice, we are to take the helmet of salvation, which is not speaking of being saved but of having assurance of salvation, so that we can be effective in witnessing and in living the daily Christian life. Satan's blows are often with a double-edged sword aimed at the head of a believer to bring about discouragement and doubt. To discourage us, Satan points to our failures, sins, unresolved problems or poor health and any other negative area of our lives.

Elijah, after a great victory on Mount Carmel, asked God to take his life. Look at Job, Jonah, and a myriad of others who have struggled with discouragement.

Then comes the broadsword of doubt: does God really understand, does He care, and am I really a child of God? We must have our helmet of salvation securely fastened with full faith in receiving the truth of God's Word.

Attacking with the Word

All of the pieces of armor have been primarily for defense and protection, but in verse 17b we find a piece of armor that is also offensive, "… and the sword of the Spirit, which is the word of God." The sword to which Paul refers here is not the large broad sword, but a smaller sword which varied in length from six to eighteen inches, carried by Roman foot soldiers into battle, and was the principal weapon in hand-to-hand combat. It was carried in a sheath or scabbard attached to the belt, always ready to be used.

It is interesting to note that the first piece of armor was the belt of truth to which the sword of truth is attached. This sword of the Word is "of the Spirit," and is our most powerful weapon because it is capable of accomplishing supernatural feats.

The Scottish Pastor and writer, Thomas Guthrie, said, "The Bible is an armory of heavenly weapons, a laboratory of infallible medicines, a mine of exhaustless wealth. It is a guide book for every road, a chart for every sea, a medicine for every malady, and a balm for every wound. Rob us of our Bible and the sky has lost its Sun."

1. The Word strengthens us for battle. Soldiers must be fit to be able to be effective in battle. Every soldier needs daily strength. (1 Peter 2:2; Hebrews 5:14; Jeremiah 15:16; Psalm 119:103)

2. The Word is used as a defensive weapon. The Roman Soldier, with his sword drawn, was able to stop the enemy attack leveled at him. Every attack to the Christian warrior can be defeated by "It is written" as Jesus proved in Matthew 4:1–11.

3. The Word is used as an offensive weapon. The soldier, as he stood in battle, not only deflected the enemies' attacks, but he used his sword to pierce through the enemy. Hebrews 4:12, "For the word of God is quick, and powerful, and sharper than any two edged sword, piercing even to the dividing asunder of soul and spirit, and of the joints and marrow, and is a discerner of the thoughts and intents of the heart."

The sword of the Word is quick, that is alive and powerful as it can penetrate anything, even to the inner depths of a man's soul; and it discerns every inner thought and intent. What a sword—this powerful weapon that can accomplish the impossible! It is essential that every Christian warrior both know and act on the Word of God to win this great battle against his enemies.

Prayer is the closing theme of the letter of Ephesians here in verse 18, and is closely related to putting on the full armor. Perhaps prayer is the seventh piece of God's armor. We are to be in an attitude of prayer at all times as Paul stated in 1 Thessalonians 5:17: "Pray without ceasing." Prayer is the spiritual air that the Christian soldier breathes. It is essential to spiritual warfare. Now prayer is the crescendo at the end of Paul's letter to us. He began with lifting us into the heavenlies, and now ends by challenging us to bow the knee. This armor of God is not mechanical or magical in nature, but it is energized by prayer. Oh, the great power of prayer and what it can accomplish!

A remarkable incident occurred some years ago when a Christian called upon God in a time of great danger. A twelve-car passenger train was speeding along in Eastern Missouri. On board were hundreds of children on their way to a special Sunday school conference. The sky was cloudless when the excursion began, but it was not long before they ran into a severe thunderstorm. The heavy downpour caused the engineer to slow down to about 35 mph.

As the train rounded a curve, the engineer and fireman saw that the switch just ahead had been left wide open. He jammed on the brakes, but there was no time to stop and certain disaster faced them. "Derail, stick with it," he shouted to the fireman, "we have hundreds of children on board." "I intend to," came the reply. The fireman, who was a Christian, dropped to his knees and cried out to God, "Oh Lord, help us; we need You." His words were almost drowned out by a loud clap of thunder as a bolt of lightning struck right in front of the train. The next thing they knew, they were safely past the danger point. After the train came to a complete stop they walked back to the switch to find out what had happened. To their amazement they discovered that the lightning bolt had struck the rails and closed the switch!

The power of prayer is readily available in any time of need and danger. James 5:16 says, "…The effectual, fervent prayer of a righteous man availeth much." In times of *testing, trial,* and *temptation,* prayer is for God's intervention and deliverance. In times of *blessing, victory,* and *fruitbearing,* prayer is for complete gratitude for God's gracious provisions. Prayer is the vital link of communication and fellowship with God, at *any time* and *all the time* is *the best time to pray.*

SUMMARY OF THIS CHAPTER

This chapter has focused on the weapons God has given the Christian and the need to put on the whole armor of God so that we can gain victory over the enemy.

    I.   The Weapon of Commitment
   II.   The Weapon of Comprehension
  III.   The Weapon of Confidence
  IV.   The Weapon of Compliance
   V.   The Weapon of Contending
  VI.   The Weapons of Conquest
      A.   Knowing the Word
      B.   Obeying the Word
      C.   Giving the Word
      D.   Believing the Word
      E.   Receiving the Word
      F.   Attacking with the Word

ACTION STEPS

Here are three action steps you can take to march in victory in the battles the Christian soldier faces. (Initial and date when completed.)

1.   Are you, here and now, experiencing regular victory? If not, what are the weapons you are missing? List them on a 3x5 card, and determine to implement them.

Initial _____ Date _____

2. Read several key verses about walking in victory found in Ephesians 6:10–11 and Hebrews 4:12. Write out on 3x5 cards and put to memory.

Initial _____ Date _____

3. Commit to make a concerted effort to pray constantly. Make a prayer list and claim the victory we have in Christ.

Initial _____ Date _____

CHAPTER SEVEN

The Man's Weights

The measure of weights a man allows in his life will
determine the heights to which he will soar spiritually.

Several years ago, my wife and I had the opportunity to take a hot air balloon ride in Southern California near Temecula. We arrived early in the morning, just before the sun came up, and we saw several balloons lying on the ground. Soon workers began to force hot air into the lower opening of a balloon, and as the hot air increased, the large, colorful balloon began to lift off of the ground. The more the hot air filled the balloon, the more it lifted up in the air. But holding down that balloon were some weights attached to its base that kept it from lifting off. We climbed aboard, and at the command of the captain, the weights were cut loose, and we began to rise above the earth. As the balloon ascended to the sky we witnessed a spectacular view of a glorious sunrise and the miles and miles of beautiful orange groves and grape vineyards that lay beneath us. What an awesome experience that was with that great panoramic view and the perfect solitude as a light breeze carried us along.

I believe God wants His men to soar and to climb to new heights in their Christian lives. Yet, certain weights in our lives keep us down. The Lord wants us to soar with eagles, not walk with turkeys, as someone has said. Isaiah said it well in Isaiah 40:31, "But they that wait upon the Lord shall renew their strength; they shall mount up with wings as eagles; they shall run and not be weary; and they shall walk and not faint." Just as the eagle was meant to fly and soar high above the earth, so we are to live on a higher plane above the limitations of this world. Several weights, however, may keep you from reaching the spiritual heights you desire.

The Apostle Paul often used athletic examples to help us understand spiritual truths. One of these examples is a foot-race in which a group of runners compete. Obviously the goal of any runner is not only to complete the race, but to win and receive the prize—today, a gold medal, but in Paul's day, a laurel crown.

First Corinthians 9:24–27 says, "Know ye not that they which run in a race run all, but one receiveth the prize? So run, that ye may obtain. And every man that striveth for the mastery is temperate in all things. Now they do it to obtain a corruptible crown; but we an incorruptible. I therefore so run, not as uncertainly; so fight I, not as one that beateth the air: But I keep under my body, and bring it into subjection: lest that by any means, when I have preached to others, I myself should be a castaway." So "man that striveth for the mastery is temperate in all things." He is self-controlled, and brings his body into subjection so that he will be in the winner's circle and not disqualified. Sins are to be forsaken. Weights or hindrances must be laid aside.

I never did compete in any track and field events in my high school or college career. However, I have watched many of these sporting events. I remember that runners often trained wearing weights to help them get conditioned for the race. However, on race days those weights were taken off. Can you imagine a runner walking up to the starting blocks still wearing training weights?

It is just as absurd to try to run the race of the Christian life with weights on.

The writer of Hebrews gives to us a tremendous challenge in Hebrews 12:1–2, "Wherefore seeing we also are compassed about with so great a cloud of witnesses, let us lay aside every weight, and the sin which doth so easily beset us, and let us run with patience the race that is set before us, Looking unto Jesus the author and finisher of our faith; who for the joy that was set before him endured the cross, despising the shame, and is set down at the right hand of the throne of God." How should we run the race of the Christian life?

The Event

First of all, the participants are you and me as born-again believers. Second, it is a race that we are to "run with patience." The word *run* carries the thought of agony—that it is often extremely difficult. Lazy Christians never win as Amos 6:1a says: "Woe to them that are at ease...." *Patience* means endurance. The Christian life is not a one-hundred-yard dash, but a lifelong marathon. We must continue running until the end of our lives, and strive to be faithful to the end.

Winners need preparation—discipline, self-denial, and self-control. We must commit to do our absolute best in all things so that we can win. Philippians 3:14 says: "I press toward the mark for the prize of the high calling of God in Christ Jesus." And 1 Corinthians 9:25 says: "And every man that striveth for the mastery is temperate in all things. Now they do it to obtain a corruptible crown; but we an incorruptible."

The Encouragement

"Wherefore seeing we also are compassed about with so great a cloud of witnesses..." (Hebrews 12:1a). This cloud of witnesses refers to the list of the heroes of the faith found in Hebrews 11. They surround us as a "great cloud" and cheer us on. I can almost hear their voices in the grandstands of Heaven saying, "Run, run! You can do it through Christ; you can complete the race just as we have; therefore continue to run for the prize."

The Encumbrances

"...let us lay aside every weight, and the sin which doth so easily beset us..." (Hebrews 12:1). One thing that you learn as you run is to run light. Every unnecessary article and unneeded piece of clothing needs to be removed, because all excess weight must be eliminated. Here are five types of weights that may hold some back. While most are not sins per se, two examples of weights that are sins are included.

Spiritual weights

There are good men who run in the Christian race with unbiblical thinking. Some may lack assurance of their salvation because they have a blurred memory of when and where they were saved. If you have any doubt or question, go back to the first part of chapter 1 on "the man's will" and settle this most important decision. Others, however, lack an understanding of eternal security, and so they fear that they may have lost, or could lose, their salvation. The simple Bible answer is that once you are truly saved, you have eternal life that cannot be lost. A great book on this theme is *Done* by Cary Schmidt, from Striving Together Publications.

Also, look at John 10:28–30, "And I give unto them eternal life; and they shall never perish, neither shall any man pluck them out of my hand. My Father, which gave them me, is greater than all; and no man is able to pluck them out of my Father's hand. I and my Father are one." And 1 John 5:11–13 says, "And this is the record, that God hath given to us eternal life, and this life is in his Son. He that hath the Son hath life; and he that hath not the Son of God hath not life. These things have I written unto you that believe on the name of the Son of God; that ye may know that ye have eternal life, and that ye may believe on the name of the Son of God." Many men struggle in their race because of the weight of doubt—a lack of assurance of their salvation.

Emotional weights

Discouragement and depression are no respecter of persons. They weigh down many men, including some of the greatest Christians as well as famous leaders throughout history. Moses, Elijah, and Jonah are examples of men in the Bible who became so depressed and overwhelmed by circumstances that they wanted to die rather than live. Charles Spurgeon suffered dark periods of anguishing depression. The preacher, John Knox, and the great missionary, Adoniram Judson, fought bouts of depression.

There are many circumstances that can cause some depression for a runner. Sometimes it is caused by overwhelming disobedience and sins, but most often it is simply a feeling of hopelessness that seems to have no obvious cause and may be due to a chemical imbalance in a runner's brain.

There is no easy, quick fix for depression; however, Psalm 42:5 says, "Why art thou cast down, O my soul? And why art thou disquieted in me? hope thou in God: for I shall yet praise him for the help of his countenance." And verse 11 says, "Why are thou cast down, O my soul? and why art thou disquieted within me? hope thou in God: for I shall yet praise him, who is the health of my countenance, and my God."

If sin is the root cause, it must be dealt with, and qualified medical assistance may help. However, our vision has often been blurred by looking at ourselves, or at others, or at the dark circumstances around us. We must turn our eyes to the Lord and trust the one who will carry us on in the race as 1 Peter 5:7 says: "Casting all your care upon him; for he careth for you." In

2 Corinthians 12:9–10 Paul said, "And he said unto me, My grace is sufficient for thee: for my strength is made perfect in weakness. Most gladly therefore will I rather glory in my infirmities, that the power of Christ may rest upon me. Therefore I take pleasure in infirmities, in reproaches, in necessities, in persecutions, in distresses for Christ's sake: for when I am weak, then am I strong."

One other debilitating emotional weight is a sin that many men struggle with—bitterness. Bitterness will impact you negatively in your walk with God, your relationships with others, your emotional stability, and your health. Bitterness, it is said, is the only chemical that destroys its own container. Confess your bitter spirit to God, and forgive whoever you feel has hurt you. Ephesians 4:31–32 says, "Let all bitterness, and wrath, and anger, and clamour, and evil speaking, be put away from you, with all malice: And be ye kind one to another, tenderhearted, forgiving one another, even as God for Christ's sake hath forgiven you."

Physical weights

There are runners who have debilitating physical weights that could slow or impair them. The Apostle Paul struggled with his thorn in the flesh. We do not know exactly what the thorn was, but he lived with pain, and his eyesight was affected. Yet this obviously did not slow him down. Jacob, in that wrestling match, was touched in the thigh by the Lord, and afterward walked with a limp.

Over my lifetime I have known of scores of God's runners who had to deal with disease, accidents, or congenital disabilities, yet they continued on in their race, maybe not as quickly, but faithfully. I found myself without a voice some years ago. My condition, called Spastic Dysphonia, was said to be incurable by the medical authorities at that time who said I would never preach again. It was a great struggle, and the thought of throwing in the towel came to my mind sometimes. I thank the Lord for His enabling grace that kept me going on in the race in those dark days. Then, by His miracle-working power, my voice was restored, and today I thank God that I'm still running the race.

We live in a society that has become somewhat obese as our diet and lack of exercise have caused many runners to struggle with their physical weight. There are certainly those who, because of thyroid conditions or some genetic background, find themselves facing an extra challenge. The Bible tells us that our bodies are God's dwelling place, 1 Corinthians 6:19–20, "What? know ye not that your body is the temple of the Holy Ghost which is in you, which ye have of God, and ye are not your own? For ye are bought with a price: therefore glorify God in your body, and in your spirit, which are God's."

The runner's overweight condition presents a poor testimony and brings a measure of injury to God's dwelling place. It is important that great effort and real commitment be given to keeping our physical weight down and "in check." Remember, to run effectively requires us to run as light as possible. Obesity is a difficult area to deal with, but it is a hindrance to the runner. Don't allow your physical weight to stop you, but rely upon the grace of God and "keep on keeping on." Philippians 4:13 says: "I can do all things through Christ which strengtheneth me."

Material weights

Materialism weighs us down greatly. We live in a materialistic society, and everything around us seems to focus upon things and possessions. I have watched faithful men who were ensnared by a promotion, a raise in income, an extra side job, or some large inheritance. There is nothing wrong with money, but 1 Timothy 6:8–10 says, "And having food and raiment let us be therewith content. But they that will be rich fall into temptation and a snare, and into many foolish and hurtful lusts, which drown men in destruction and perdition. For the love of money is the root of all evil: which while some coveted after, they have erred from the faith, and pierced themselves through with many sorrows."

God often blesses us with "things" and material possessions; however, you must not allow these earthly possessions to possess you. Keep your eyes on the Lord as Paul said in Philippians 3:14, "I press toward the mark for the prize of the high calling of God in Christ Jesus." The Lord tells us to keep our eyes only on Him and on eternity. Colossians 3:1–2 says, "If ye then be risen with Christ, seek those things which are above, where Christ sitteth on the right hand of God. Set your affection on things above, not on things on the earth."

Many men, while running the race, have found themselves and their families in ruin because they got off of the main track and ran towards material goals. Earthly things last for only a fleeting moment, as money has wings and flies away, and possessions rot, rust, and decay.

As Jesus said in Matthew 6:19–21, "Lay not up for yourselves treasures upon earth, where moth and rust doth corrupt, and where thieves break through and steal: But lay up for yourselves treasures in heaven, where neither moth nor rust doth corrupt, and where thieves do not break through nor steal: For where your treasure is, there will your heart be also." Invest in eternity, and do not get your roots down too deep here on earth, for your real home is in Heaven.

Recreational weights

There are few who do not enjoy some kind of sport or recreational activity. Most enjoy the challenge of competing to win and engaging in some kind of athletic activity such as golfing, hunting, fishing, boating, camping, etc. Paul often used sporting terms and language to depict some aspects of the Christian life.

Being involved in various forms of recreation and having outlets are not necessarily wrong in themselves. However, they can become weights and hindrances to a man running the race. Just being a spectator—reading the sports page, watching TV sports, or attending some game—can be a weight or hindrance. We spend both money and time on these things rather than investing in Christ and His work.

Perhaps sports and recreation, while not evil in themselves, cause us to miss church and/or limit or end our service to Christ. Don't allow something that may be good become a weight and therefore possibly a sin in your life. Many men spend hours in front of a TV as a "couch potato," or become consumed with the computer or video games. All of these are fine in moderation. However, if we are spending lots of time in these activities when we could be tending to spiritual or family responsibilities, we have weighed ourselves down.

Evaluate where you spend your money and how much time you invest away from your wife, your family, and your local church. Your job takes enough of your time. Strive for things that are excellent. As Philippians 1:10 says: "That ye may approve things that are excellent; that ye may be sincere and without offence till the day of Christ."

These five areas of weights have limited many men who could have won the crown and finished the race, honoring the coach of the team, the Lord Jesus Christ. Determine to lay aside any and all weights that hold you back and hinder you from effectively running the race.

The Example

Look again at Hebrews 12:2, "Looking unto Jesus the author and finisher of our faith; who for the joy that was set before him endured the cross, despising the shame, and is set down at the right hand of the throne of God." This is our pattern, the example we are to follow. Thank God for many faithful and godly men around us, yet the one who never fails and who is far, far out front in this race is Jesus Christ.

His faith

We are to look to and focus upon Him as Hebrews says, "Looking unto Jesus...." The word *looking* conveys the thought of looking intently or giving full attention. Jesus is the author, the originator, and the captain of our faith. He is also the finisher. Thank God He victoriously completed His race as He stated in John 17:4: "I have glorified thee on the earth: I have finished the work which thou gavest me to do." The Lord Jesus demonstrated commitment, faithfulness, and faith over and over again. Amen!

His focus

"...who for the joy that was set before him endured the cross, despising the shame...." Even before the foundations of the earth were laid in the council of the godhead, Jesus was destined for the Cross. Born of a virgin, He lived a sinless, perfect life. He encountered opposition, temptations, trials, betrayal, beatings, and finally, the Cross. In running the race He never flinched but fixed His eye, like a flint, upon His goal, the Cross.

Isaiah said in chapter 50:6–7, "I gave my back to the smiters, and my cheeks to them that plucked off the hair: I hid not my face from shame and spitting. For the Lord GOD will help me; therefore shall I not be confounded: therefore have I set my face like a flint, and I know that I shall not be ashamed." Jesus was focused on fulfilling the Father's call and finished His race victoriously.

His finish

"...is set down at the right hand of the throne of God." The word *finish* literally means to carry through to completion. On Calvary, paying for our sin, He cried out, "It is finished" as He accomplished the work of redemption. Now He is "set down" because He finished His race. Hebrews 1:3 says, "Who being the brightness of his glory, and the express image of his person, and upholding all things by the word of his power, when he had by himself purged our sins, sat down on the right hand of the Majesty on high." He is seated at the right hand of the Father now, and when our race is over one day, we too can rest.

You may say, "Well, I have fallen out of the race, and I just don't think I can finish." I challenge you to get up and lay aside your excuses and weights and get back in the race! Proverbs 24:16 says: "For a just man falleth seven times, and riseth up again: but the wicked shall fall into mischief." There is much at stake, not only in your life, but in the lives of those who watch you run. The grace of God and His strength and power will enable you, but you must be willing to lay aside every weight and the sin that so easily besets us.

> On March 6, 1987, Eamon Coughlan, the Irish world record holder at 1,500 meters, was running in a qualifying heat at the World Indoor Track Championships in Indianapolis. With two and a half laps left, he was tripped. He fell, but he got up and with great effort managed to catch the leaders. With only 20 yards left in the race, he was in third place, good enough to qualify for the finals. He looked over his shoulder to the inside, and, seeing no one, he let up. But another runner, charging hard on the outside, passed Coughlan a yard before the finish, and thus eliminated him from the finals. Coughlan's great comeback effort was rendered worthless because he took his eyes off the finish line. It's tempting to let up when things around us look favorable. But we finish well in the Christian race only when we fix our eyes on the goal: Jesus Christ. (source unknown)

SUMMARY OF THIS CHAPTER

This chapter has focused on the many weights that will hinder any man from running the race in the Christian life. Keep on running, and stay focused on your captain.

    I.   The Event
   II.   The Encouragement
  III.   The Encumbrances
        A.   Spiritual weights
        B.   Emotional weights
        C.   Physical weights
        D.   Material weights
        E.   Recreational weights
   IV.   The Example
        A.   His faith
        B.   His focus
        C.   His finish

ACTION STEPS

Here are three action steps you can take to run the race faithfully and to be victorious in the winner's circle. (Initial and date when completed.)

1.   Take a 3x5 card and write out Hebrews 12:1–2 and put it to memory.

   Initial _____ Date _____

2.   Think of some key weights that may have hindered your running the race, and write these out on paper,

committing these to the Lord. Determine to lay them aside.

Initial _____ Date _____

3. List, on a card, at least fifteen people watching you run your race, and focus on being the right kind of an example to those around you.

Initial _____ Date _____

CHAPTER EIGHT

The Man's Woes

*The trials and adversities of life can tend to defeat
us, but in actuality they should be tools to mold us,
mature us, and propel us to greater heights.*

In this chapter, we will consider times of trial and hardship,
because every man will eventually face some of these woes. Job
said in Job 5:7, "Yet man is born unto trouble, as the sparks
fly upward," and again in Job 14:1, "Man that is born of a woman
is of few days, and full of trouble." It was said of the Messiah in
Isaiah 53:3, "He is despised and rejected of men; a man of sorrows,
and acquainted with grief: and we hid as it were our faces from
him; he was despised, and we esteemed him not."

Each of us endures some trouble; it is the consequence of
the fall of man, the natural result of this wicked world and of our
sinful nature. However, we will see that behind the scenes, God has
planned to use the trial for our good and His glory.

Years ago a fishing fleet went out from a small harbor on the
east coast of Newfoundland. In the afternoon, a tremendous storm
arose. By nightfall, not a single vessel of all the fleet had found its
way to the safe harbor. All night long, families, sweethearts, and

friends paced up and down the beach peering into the darkness, praying that God would save their loved ones and friends. Adding to their burdens, one of the cottages along the shore caught fire. Since all of the men were at sea, there was no one to save the home.

When morning finally broke, to the great joy of all, the entire fleet sailed safely back into the small harbor. The entire village was elated as the men walked up the pier to the waiting families and friends. However, one wife stood with tears streaming down her face with a look of despair. As she threw her arms around her husband's neck, she cried, "O husband, we are ruined, our home burned to the ground last night." "Oh thank God," exclaimed the husband, "My dear, it was the light of our burning cottage that guided the entire fleet back home to safety."

Often God's purpose is to use the great trials in our lives to help others. Romans 8:28 says, "And we know that all things work together for good to them that love God, to them who are the called according to his purpose." We cannot really understand God's omnipotence or omniscience. Isaiah 55:8–9 says; "For my thoughts are not your thoughts, neither are your ways my ways, saith the LORD. For as the heavens are higher than the earth, so are my ways higher than your ways, and my thoughts than your thoughts." Nevertheless we must try to comprehend His attributes.

Matthew Arnold, a Christian writer of the nineteenth century, wrote a book entitled *Sweetness and Light*. Unfortunately, life is not all sweetness and light, although we wish it were. Many Christians have been led to believe a "Pollyanna'" gospel: that is, when a person comes to Christ, all the problems and troubles of life will vanish. Those who believe that teaching have been sold a falsehood.

Many Christian men have found themselves with great trials and have become broken emotionally. A theologian of the Middle Ages, John of the Cross, called these times "the dark night of the soul." We wonder what has happened. Where has God gone? And we feel that His presence has disappeared. The Bible is filled with the testimonies of many men who faced enormous difficulties and sorrows.

Job is probably the best example of a man who endeavored to live a godly life. Job 1:1 says: "There was a man in the land of Uz, whose name was Job; and that man was perfect and upright, and one that feared God, and eschewed evil." Yet Job plummeted into a black pit. Twenty-six times he used the word *darkness*.

For example, Job 17:13 says, "If I wait, the grave is mine house: I have made my bed in the darkness." And in Job 19:8 he says: "He hath fenced up my way that I cannot pass, and he hath set darkness in my paths." Yet in the loss of all his earthly possessions, his ten children, his health and the sympathy of his wife who stated in chapter 2:9, "…curse God, and die," he could still cry out in Job 13:15, "Though he slay me, yet will I trust in him: but I will maintain mine own ways before him."

John the Baptist, the forerunner of our Lord, was totally devoted to his Lord. Jesus said of him in Luke 7:28, "For I say unto you, Among those that are born of women there is not a greater prophet than John the Baptist: but he that is least in the kingdom of God is greater than he." John was arrested for preaching his convictions and put in prison. John did not understand why Jesus would allow him to linger in that dingy cell. He even sent out two of his disciples to find out if Jesus was really the Messiah or if they should look for someone else. John was beheaded, and never knew why God apparently abandoned him.

Despairing under the weight of painful trials, many have asked "Why? Why is this happening to me? Why now?" In those times of darkness the question to ask is not "Why?" but rather, "What does God want me to learn from this?" Remember that stars only appear in darkness, and the darker the night the brighter their beauty and brilliance. The stars are there all the time, but only night will reveal them.

The book, *A View from the Bottom of the Well*, states that if you are in a deep, dark well in daytime, you can look up and see the stars shining. Perhaps God lets us endure darkness because we have become dazzled by the brightness of this world. He wants us to turn our eyes to Heaven and see His radiance. No matter how dark the night or deep the trial, darkness turns to daylight, and we will emerge into that light.

Remember Psalm 30:5, "For his anger endureth but a moment; in his favour is life: weeping may endure for a night, but joy cometh in the morning." The same sun that sets every evening will rise again every morning. Dark times are normal, fruitful, and temporary. Through them all, our Redeemer is always there as He said in Hebrews 13:5: "…I will never leave thee, nor forsake thee."

We can trust Him who is invisible but ever present. His promises remain sure. Warren Wiersbe stated, "We don't live by explanations, we live by promises. God is under no obligation to tell us 'why' or explain Himself, for even if He did, we probably would not even grasp it."

Romans 11:33–36 states: "O the depth of the riches both of the wisdom and knowledge of God! how unsearchable are his judgments, and his ways past finding out! For who hath known the mind of the Lord? or who hath been his counsellor? Or who hath first given to him, and it shall be recompensed unto him again? For of him, and through him, and to him, are all things: to whom be glory for ever. Amen." Thomas Watson commented, "Where reason cannot wade, faith must swim."

So when these troubles come along, look to the Lord first, keep on praying, reading your Bible and serving Him. Then lean on the Lord and rest in His arms of safety. As Proverbs 3:5–6 states: "Trust in the Lord with all thine heart; and lean not unto thine own understanding. In all thy ways acknowledge him, and he shall direct thy paths." Sometimes the Lord has to take away everything we depend on to help us learn to lean on Him.

Finally, leave it with the Lord. Our attitude may be, "I'm going to do something, even if it is wrong." If you "grab the bull by the horns," you will probably get gored; so do not take matters into your own hands. The Bible is full of unfortunate examples of those who took matters into their own hands. Abraham, even after the Lord had promised him a son many times, took matters into his own hands. He and Sarah could not wait, and Ishmael was born by Sarah's handmaid, and Isaac's descendants are still fighting with the descendants of Ishmael. "…wait, I say, on the Lord" (Psalm 27:14).

Impetuous Peter, a take-matters-into-my-own-hands kind of man, with good intentions, ended up cutting off the ear of Malchus, the servant of the high priest. Jesus rebuked him, and let him know that He could have called a legion of angels to deliver Him at a moment's notice. Do not ruin your life or the lives of others, but look to the Lord, lean on the Lord, and leave it with the Lord.

The cocoon of the Emperor moth is flask shaped. In order for this beautiful, perfect insect to emerge, it must force its way through the extremely narrow neck of the cocoon by hours of intense struggling. It is believed that the pressure to which the moth's body is subjected is a provision of nature for forcing the insect's fluids into the vessels of the wings, thus producing a beautiful winged Emperor moth.

One day, a well-meaning individual was watching this struggle and out of pity took some scissors and snipped off some of the confining threads. Those threads seemed to be hindering the moth's escape, and the individual wanted to make it easier for the moth to be freed from the cocoon. However, the moth's wings never developed, and it spent its brief life-span crawling on the ground instead of soaring through the air using its beautiful rainbow wings. Out of struggles, we develop the strength to soar to new heights by His grace. We may not always understand God's reasons, but these reasons exist.

I remember that several years ago, my neighbor was in his backyard doing some work. I called out, "What are you up to today?" to which he replied, "I'm pruning my apricot trees." He said he had just taken a class and found out he had been pruning all wrong. He commented that the previous year he had lost several trees, and the rest did not bear much fruit. I asked what he was doing differently, to which he said he had been too easy on his trees and failed to prune them back far enough. He stated, "I'm cutting them way back because I must hurt my trees in order to help my trees."

That is exactly what our Master must sometimes do to us because the Husbandman wants us to bear more fruit. Here are some possible reasons for our trials. James 1:2–4 says, "My brethren, count it all joy when ye fall into divers temptations; Knowing this, that the trying of your faith worketh patience. But let patience have her perfect work, that ye may be perfect and entire, wanting nothing." He wants us to be *perfect*, which means mature and complete.

Trials Strengthen Our Faith

Often troubles can reveal the measure of our faith. Proverbs 24:10 says, "If thou faint in the day of adversity, thy strength is small." But trials can also strengthen our faith. Do not become resentful or bitter, for doing so reveals your weak faith.

The writer of 2 Chronicles 32:31 said this about Hezekiah: "…God left him, to try him, that he might know all that was in his heart." The truth is that the Lord already knows what is in our hearts, but trials reveal to us the level of our faith. David said in Psalm 139:23, "Search me, O God, and know my heart: try me, and know my thoughts." The Lord already knew, but David needed to know his own heart's faith.

Trials Are Given to Humble Us

One of the greatest hindrances to fellowship with the Lord is pride. James 4:6–7, 10 states: "But he giveth more grace. Wherefore he saith, God resisteth the proud, but giveth grace unto the humble. Submit yourselves therefore to God. Resist the devil, and he will flee from you. Humble yourselves in the sight of the Lord, and he shall lift you up." When things are going great we become self-sufficient and proud. It was the first king, Saul, who was tall and handsome. He became filled with pride and failed the test over Agag and the Amalekites, and God rejected him.

I remember watching the Winter Olympics snowboarding finals several years ago. As the four finalists traversed down the course, the competition was intense. Lindsey Jacobellis, an American, took a commanding lead. Way out in front, she decided on the last jump to strut her stuff and "hot dog" it. She did a backside air grab and lost her balance and fell, losing the gold to Swiss snowboarder, Tanya Frieden.

First Corinthians 10:12 says, "Wherefore let him that thinketh he standeth take heed lest he fall." Trials are often the tool used to humble us.

Trials Reveal What We Really Love

What has our affections? Trials can come along to hurt or destroy what we hold most dear. We are to love the Lord most of all, according to Matthew 22:37: "Jesus said unto him, Thou shalt love the Lord thy God with all thy heart, and with all thy soul, and with all thy mind." Material things and worldly pleasures must be removed, for they take our focus from the Lord.

Sometimes we need to sacrifice good things. Remember that Abraham climbed up that mountain with the promised heir, his beloved son Isaac. Genesis 22:9–10 recounts: "And they came to the place which God had told him of; and Abraham built an altar there, and laid the wood in order, and bound Isaac his son, and laid him on the altar upon the wood. And Abraham stretched forth his hand, and took the knife to slay his son." Here was a real test. Abraham was willing to sacrifice even his precious son Isaac. Trials often reveal what we love the most—God, or something or someone else.

Trials Direct Us to Our Heavenly Home

We often become too attached to the world and our earthly homes, but trials can help us see our real home in Heaven. We are strangers and pilgrims down here because our real citizenship is in Heaven. According to Philippians 3:20: "For our conversation is in heaven; from whence also we look for the Saviour, the Lord Jesus Christ."

We often sing, "This world is not my home I'm just a-passing through; my treasures are laid up somewhere beyond the blue." Trials can help us understand that we should not be too attached to this world. Paul expressed it well in Philippians 1:23: "For I am in a strait betwixt two, having a desire to depart, and to be with Christ; which is far better."

Trials Develop and Mature Saints

The Lord is always at work to mature us, usually through trials. When we come to the end of ourselves in times of difficulty, we finally realize His strength. Paul says in 2 Corinthians 12:10: "Therefore I take pleasure in infirmities, in reproaches, in necessities, in persecutions, in distresses for Christ's sake: for when I am weak, then am I strong."

There is little growth on the high mountaintop because fruit grows best in the valleys. Trouble is one of the ways of pruning that God uses. Charles Spurgeon said, "There are some of your graces which would never be discovered if it were not for your trials. God often removes our comforts and our privileges in order to make us better Christians. He trains His soldiers, not in tents of ease and luxury, but by turning them out and pushing them to forced marches and hard service. He has them ford through streams, swim through rivers, climb mountains, and walk many a long mile with heavy knapsacks on their backs."

Could God's pruning account for the troubles you are experiencing? Is the Lord bringing out your graces and making them grow? Is this the reason He seems to be contending with you?

Trials Enable Us to Minister to Others

We can minister to others more effectively when we have been confronted by similar circumstances. Jesus spoke to Peter and challenged him to minister to others after he had gone through testing. Luke 22:31–32 says, "And the Lord said, Simon, Simon, behold, Satan hath desire to have you, that he may sift you as wheat: But I have prayed for thee, that thy faith fail not: and when thou art converted, strengthen thy brethren." I realize that some of my trials have enabled me to minister to others. Great health problems, a loss of possessions, the death of a loved one, and other difficulties may enable us to aid others with similar problems.

In 2 Corinthians 1:3–4 Paul says, "Blessed be God, even the Father of our Lord Jesus Christ, the Father of mercies, and the God of all comfort: Who comforteth us in all our tribulation, that we may be able to comfort them which are in any trouble, by the comfort wherewith we ourselves are comforted of God."

We can be most effective after trials; Jesus endured suffering so He can now come to our aid and comfort us. Hebrews 2:18: "For in that he himself hath suffered being tempted, he is able to succour them that are tempted." Trials make us uniquely prepared to aid others.

I heard the story of a man hiking in the mountains, when suddenly he fell off the side of a cliff. About twenty feet down he was able to grab hold of a limb jutting out of the side of the mountain. Looking down, he could see the jagged rocks about 1,000 feet below. Seeing his plight, he cried out, "HELP ME, HELP ME! PLEASE, SOMEBODY, HELP ME!" Suddenly a voice came back, "I hear you, and I can help you. I am the Lord, just trust me, and let go of the limb. Trust me." The man, looked down again at the jagged rocks 1,000 feet below, and then he looked up again and called out, "Is there anyone else up there?"

This is an amusing story, but in fact, when trials, troubles and testing come, rather than trusting the Lord, we hang onto the weak limb, and cry out, "Is there anyone else who can help me?" An all-caring, all-sufficient, all-wise Heavenly Father who knows our situation and cares beyond our understanding permits the trials we go through. God is much more interested in the man than in the man's ministry. If the Lord can somehow get our attention, then our ministry will be right. In conclusion:

There is a purpose for trials.

Everything God allows to come across our paths has a purpose and a reason even though we may not always understand why.

There is provision in trials.

God's grace is always sufficient; He will give us just what we need when we need it. Spurgeon said, "Man's extremity is God's opportunity." God brings us to the point of desperation to bring us to the point of dependence, which will bring us to the point of deliverance.

There is power in the trial.

It was said of King Uzziah that he was marvelously helped until he was strong. God gives strength and power to the weak. Isaiah 40:29 says, "He giveth power to the faint; and to them that have no might he increaseth strength."

There is pleasure in trials.

When God sovereignly allowed the messenger of Satan to buffet Paul with his thorn in the flesh, Satan's intent was to defeat Paul.

However, Paul humbled himself, and the thorn was turned into triumph. Note Paul's statement in 2 Corinthians 12:10, "Therefore I take pleasure in infirmities, in reproaches, in necessities, in persecutions, in distresses for Christ's sake: for when I am weak, then am I strong."

A new, sweet and deep relationship with Christ is developed through trials. Whatever trials or troubles come your way, turn them over to the Lord; trust Him; and allow Him to use them for your good and His glory. First Peter 1:7 states: "That the trial of your faith, being much more precious than of gold that perisheth, though it be tried with fire, might be found unto praise and honour and glory at the appearing of Jesus Christ."

SUMMARY OF THIS CHAPTER

This chapter is to help us face our trials, go through them, and then come out better than we were before.

I. Trials Strengthen Our Faith
II. Trials Are Given to Humble Us
III. Trials Reveal What We Really Love
IV. Trials Direct Us to Our Heavenly Home
V. Trials Develop and Mature His Saints
VI. Trials Enable Us to Minister to Others
   A. There is a purpose for trials.
   B. There is provision in trials.
   C. There is power in the trial.
   D. There is pleasure in trials.

ACTION STEPS

Here are three action steps you can take to grow in times of trial and trouble. (Initial and date when completed.)

1. List on a piece of paper what trials you have gone through that enable you to minister to others.

   Initial _____ Date _____

2. Write out on a 3x5 card the verse in 1 Peter 1:7, and put it to memory.

   Initial _____ Date _____

3. Think through what steps you plan to take when you face the next trial, and list them on a 3x5 card.

   Initial _____ Date _____

CHAPTER NINE

The Man's Warriors

The bond of friendship has carried many faltering warriors,
even in the midst of great challenges and impossible conditions.

I n a world filled with so much turmoil, one of the great blessings
for any warrior is to have those around him whom he can call
"friend." Everyone needs a friend, a fellow soldier on whom he
can lean and in whom he can confide in times of need. I am very
glad for those special men in my life that I can call "my friends."

The book, *How to Win Friends and Influence People*, has sold
millions of copies because we recognize that friendship is very
important. Another book by McGinniss, entitled *The Friendship
Factor*, has also been a bestseller. Not all books, however, are about
real friendship because they teach us only how to get close to
people that we love, to give them attention and affirmation. Real
friendships, as a rule, are not born by setting out to win friends.
Friendships grow from knowing people who have a kindred spirit
and see things as you do.

I remember hearing an evangelist state that if, after a lifetime,
as you lie on your deathbed, you can gather seven real friends

around you, you have been successful. I have many, many men I can call "my friends." But, as I reflect on those people that I can call real, true-blue friends, they are few indeed! A cynical but true saying often repeated in our nation's capitol is, "If you want a friend in Washington D.C., get yourself a dog."

Having real committed friends is sometimes difficult, but remember Proverbs 18:24, "A man that hath friends must shew himself friendly...." Some men make enemies instead of friends because it is easier. Friendships require time and attention, but the extra effort will produce long-lasting and deep friendships. This poem says it all:

> I went out to find a friend
> But could not find one there
> I went out to be a friend
> And friends were everywhere.

A few years ago, at the Seattle Special Olympics, nine contestants, all physically or mentally disabled, assembled at the starting line for the one-hundred-yard dash. At the sound of the gun, they all started out, in not exactly a dash, but with the goal of running the race to the finish line and winning. All, that is, except one young runner who stumbled on the asphalt, tumbled over a couple of times, and began to cry. The other eight runners heard the sorrowful cry of the fallen boy. They slowed down and looked back, and then they all turned around and went to the side of their fallen companion. One girl with Down's Syndrome, bent down and kissed him and said, "This will make it better." Then all nine linked arms and walked together to the finish line.

Everyone in the stadium stood. The cheering went on for some time. The people who were there will never forget what they witnessed that day. Why? Because deep down, they knew one thing: what matters in this life more than winning for ourselves is helping others to the winner's circle. This is what real friendship is all about, even if it means slowing down and changing course to be a friend.

An English publication offered a prize for the best definition of a true friend, and they received thousands of responses. The winning definition was, "A real friend is the one who comes in when the whole world has gone out." It has been said, "If you really want to know who your friends are, just make a mistake." Here are three key factors of real friendship:

Be a Friend—Proverbs 18:24, "A man that hath friends must shew himself friendly…." Cultivate friendships with people, and be a friend to others.

Be Loyal—Proverbs 17:17, "A friend loveth at all times…." Don't be a "fair-weather friend," but stand by your friends.

Be Honest—One great test of true friendship is that you would be willing to be honest and open with your friends. Proverbs 27:5–6 says, "Open rebuke is better than secret love. Faithful are the wounds of a friend…." Real friends will listen to the correction of another without being hurt or resentful. Real friends will try to correct an erring friend because they really care.

The Word of God has much to say about the subject of friendship, and there are many examples of it in the Bible.

The Kinds of Friendships

The forgiving friend

I am so glad that Jesus was this sinner's friend. The Saviour in Luke 7:34 was "…a friend of publicans and sinners!" John 15:13–15 says, "Greater love hath no man than this, that a man lay down his life for his friends. Ye are my friends, if ye do whatsoever I command you. Henceforth I call you not servants; for the servant knoweth not what his lord doeth: but I have called you friends; for all things that I have heard of my Father I have made known unto you."

Jesus uses the vine and the branches as a means to explain the relationship we are to enjoy in Him. He states that He is the true vine, and, when we come to Him in faith as our Saviour, we are joined to Him as a branch. John 14:6 says, "Jesus saith unto him, I am the way, the truth, and the life: no man cometh unto the Father, but by me." We draw strength, courage and life from Him. In John 15:13 our Friend lays down His life for us, His friends.

John 10:10 says, "The thief cometh not, but for to steal, and to kill, and to destroy: I am come that they might have life, and that they might have it more abundantly." If you miss this friendship, you have missed the greatest friendship of all. He gave His life for me; He carries me through my life; He shares His truth with me; and He considers me His friend. Truly He is "a friend that sticketh closer than a brother" (Proverbs 18:24).

The fulfilling friend

Today, the lives of many men who know the Lord lack fulfillment because, while they have accepted Jesus Christ as their Saviour, a real friendship has never developed. Remember, friendship is not a "one-way street."

James 2:23 says of Abraham, "And the scripture was fulfilled which saith, Abraham believed God, and it was imputed unto him for righteousness: and he was called the Friend of God." Abram was a heathen from a heathen society, but as the Lord revealed Himself to him, he believed God and followed Him by faith: Genesis 12:1, 4a, "Now the LORD had said unto Abram, Get thee out of thy country, and from thy kindred, and from thy father's house, unto a land that I will shew thee...So Abram departed, as the LORD had spoken unto him...." God spoke and Abram obediently followed and thus became "a friend of God."

Remember what Jesus said in John 15:14, "Ye are my friends, if ye do whatsoever I command you." Determine to be a friend of God, and not a friend to this world. James 4:4 says, "Ye adulterers and adulteresses, know ye not that the friendship of the world is enmity with God? whosoever therefore will be a friend of the world is the enemy of God." Confess sin; turn away from worldly habits, attitudes and activities; and be a friend of God.

The fickle friend

Job walked with God obediently as he was "perfect and upright, and one that feared God, and eschewed evil" (Job 1:1). After having been wonderfully blessed with ten children, great possessions, and good health, he lost everything in a moment of time and found himself covered with boils and sitting in an ash heap. He had friends who knew what had happened and came to his side to comfort him: Job 2:11, "Now when Job's three friends heard of all this evil that was come upon him, they came every one from his own place; Eliphaz the Temanite, and Bildad the Shuhite, and Zophar the Naamathite: for they had made an appointment together to come to mourn with him and to comfort him."

These friends who came to comfort Job soon began to criticize him. While a real friend's criticism of obvious sin may help us to repent, these men condemned Job for what he had not done. He had no open sin and his trials were not punishment for sin. They hurt rather than helped Job. Moreover, they were profoundly wrong in their judgments. God later said so in Job 42:7, "…ye have not spoken of me the thing that is right, as my servant Job hath."

Be careful of fickle and critical friends. As the old saying goes, "If you lie down with the dogs, you will probably get fleas." If you spend time with fickle and critical friends, you will be hurt, and you may become like them.

The flawed friend

There are many testimonies of friendship that ruined lives. Proverbs 13:20 says, "He that walketh with wise men shall be wise: but a companion of fools shall be destroyed." We find such an account in the life of a man called Amnon, David's son, who had a friend named Jonadab. Second Samuel 13:2–3 says, "And Amnon was so vexed, that he fell sick for his sister Tamar; for she was a virgin; and Amnon thought it hard for him to do any thing to her. But Amnon had a friend, whose name was Jonadab, the son of Shimeah David's brother: and Jonadab was a very subtil man."

This friend of Amnon was a very subtle man—very cunning and deceitful. Amnon had a half-sister named Tamar, and he was extremely infatuated with her, to the point he felt sick because of his lust for her. It was this wicked friend Jonadab's vile plan that helped Amnon violate his half-sister. The rape brought about Amnon's own death when his half-brother, Absalom, Tamar's full brother, killed him. Many other tragic consequences came about because of this sinful deed.

First Corinthians 15:33, "Be not deceived: evil communications corrupt good manners." How many lives have been damaged and destroyed by wrong and wicked friends? The road to destruction is lined with many who had been traveling the right direction, but "flawed friends" turned them to the path of destruction. Proverbs 1:10–11, 15 says, "My son, if sinners entice thee, consent thou not. If they say, Come with us, let us lay wait for blood, let us lurk privily for the innocent without cause...My son, walk not thou in the way with them; refrain thy foot from their path." Avoid wicked, flawed friends.

The Keys to Friendship

The friendship of Ruth and Naomi and of Paul and Silas are two examples of friendships, but the friendship that stands out the most is that of David and Jonathan. This friendship grew during conflict and war.

The true story is told of two young men in the First World War who had been friends since childhood. They played together, went to school together, engaged in some athletic programs together, hunted and fished together, and finally, enlisted in the

Army together. Fate determined that they would eventually be in the same battle theatre together. After a particularly bitter, fierce battle, one of the friends was missing somewhere between the lines in "no man's land." The other boy, safe and unharmed, heard that his friend was missing. He went to the commanding officer and requested permission to go out and look for his friend. He was told it was no use because no one would be alive after such a severe and lengthy battle.

Not taking "no" for an answer, the young man was finally, reluctantly given permission to go seek his friend. Some time later he returned back to camp with the limp body of his friend over his shoulder. The commander said, "See, didn't I tell you it was no use to go," to which the young man replied, "But it was worth it, as I got there in time to see his smile and hear him whisper, 'I knew you'd come.'" The bond of true friendship is stronger than life.

The path of David took him from tending his father's flock of sheep to being anointed king of Israel in 1 Samuel 16. Then, in chapter 17, he went from delivering food and supplies to his brothers at the front lines of battle to delivering a nation out of the hand of the Philistines by defeating the giant Goliath. The victory made him a national hero instantaneously. King Saul was greatly impressed. David faced many challenges; however, God gave David something worth its weight in gold. He gave David a soul brother, or a kindred spirit, Jonathan, Saul's son and heir.

The writer of 1 Samuel 18:1 says, "And it came to pass, when he had made an end of speaking unto Saul, that the soul of Jonathan was knit with the soul of David, and Jonathan loved him as his own soul." Jonathan had been watching all of these events unfold, and a real friendship developed. Jonathan's soul was "knit" to David, and Jonathan loved him. The word *knit* carries the idea of "being woven together, like strands of rope 'intertwined.'"

It is interesting to note that Jonathan was about forty years of age, and David was around nineteen to twenty years old. Yet, in spite of the age difference, the Lord caused Jonathan to love and admire David. Thus David had an intimate friend in Saul's house, and Saul would soon be his enemy. This friendship existed right under King Saul's nose because Jonathan was a loyal, trusted friend to him. Here are some keys to the real, lasting friendship between these two warriors.

Similar interests

In any real relationship with others, one key ingredient is shared interests. Amos 3:3 asks: "Can two walk together, except they be agreed?" As we have already seen, David was a warrior and showed great courage in the face of the enemy. First Samuel 17:48–49 says, "And it came to pass, when the Philistine arose, and came and drew nigh to meet David, that David hastened, and ran toward the army to meet the Philistine. And David put his hand in his bag, and took thence a stone, and slang it, and smote the Philistine in his forehead, that the stone sunk into his forehead; and he fell upon his face to the earth."

Jonathan also showed great courage and was a mighty warrior. According to 1 Samuel 14:13–14, "And Jonathan climbed up upon his hands and upon his feet, and his armourbearer after him: and they fell before Jonathan; and his armourbearer slew after him. And that first slaughter, which Jonathan and his armourbearer made, was about twenty men, within as it were an half acre of land, which a yoke of oxen might plow."

These two men also showed a great love and awe for their Lord as both realized that God was glorified as they turned to worship and praise the Lord. As warriors, they both understood the victory was God's. Without question, one of the great keys to any strong friendship or relationship is similar interests.

Sacrificial giving

These two friends committed to one another through a covenant, as 1 Samuel 18:3–4 says, "Then Jonathan and David made a covenant, because he loved him as his own soul. And Jonathan stripped himself of the robe that was upon him, and gave it to David, and his garments, even to his sword, and to his bow, and to his girdle." In this covenant these two gave themselves unreservedly to one another. Now Jonathan, in token of his whole-hearted commitment, strips himself of his robe, his sword, his bow and his girdle, the waistband holding his weapons.

It is important to note that Jonathan took off the princely robe that was a symbol of authority in Israel. Jonathan recognized and acknowledged that his dear friend would be the next king of Israel. First Samuel 23:17 says: "And he said unto him, Fear not: for the hand of Saul my father shall not find thee; and thou shalt be king over Israel, and I shall be next unto thee; and that also Saul my father knoweth." Here is the son of King Saul, heir to the throne stating, "David, you are the next king of Israel" without any jealousy. A vital key to friendships is exhibiting a genuine sacrificial spirit by which we give ourselves wholly to our friend.

Steadfast loyalty

Friendships last as long as our loyalty to our friend does. When pressures arise, friendships are strained. David's greatest enemy was the father of his dearest friend. There were times when the bitterness of King Saul erupted into rage so that even Jonathan's life was threatened. First Samuel 20:30, 33 states: "Then Saul's anger was kindled against Jonathan, and he said unto him, Thou son of the perverse rebellious woman, do not I know that thou hast chosen the son of Jesse to thine own confusion, and unto the confusion of thy mother's nakedness?…And Saul cast a javelin at him to smite him: whereby Jonathan knew that it was determined of his father to slay David."

I'm so glad I have a friend, Jesus, who died for me. As John 15:13 says: "Greater love hath no man than this, that a man lay down his life for his friends." Conflict will test loyalty and show whether it is real. As Proverbs 17:17 states: "A friend loveth at all times, and a brother is born for adversity." If you are loyal to your friends, you will find a more powerful bond.

Strengthening influence

In hard times, friendships shine as a light in the gloom. On several occasions Jonathan stood up for his dear friend David. First Samuel 19:4–5 states: "And Jonathan spake good of David unto Saul his father, and said unto him, Let not the king sin against his servant, against David; because he hath not sinned against thee, and because his works have been to thee-ward very good: For he did put his life in his hand, and slew the Philistine, and the LORD wrought a great salvation for all Israel: thou sawest it, and didst rejoice: wherefore then wilt thou sin against innocent blood, to slay David without a cause?"

True friends stand up for one another and choose not to tear one another down with any gossip, the epitome of hypocrisy. Proverbs 27:17 states: "Iron sharpeneth iron; so a man sharpeneth the countenance of his friend." Never be ashamed of a true friend; speak well of him.

Remember, Satan is the accuser of the brethren, but the Lord Jesus is our friend interceding for us at the right hand of the Father. We should stand up for the Lord Jesus, our friend. Second Timothy 1:8 says, "Be not thou therefore ashamed of the testimony of our Lord, nor of me his prisoner: but be thou partaker of the afflictions of the gospel according to the power of God."

Sensitivity to needs

Jonathan was always alert to David's needs, ready to meet those needs, no matter the cost. First Samuel 20:3–4 says: "And David sware moreover, and said, Thy father certainly knoweth that I have found grace in thine eyes; and he saith, Let not Jonathan know this, lest he be grieved: but truly as the LORD liveth, and as thy soul liveth, there is but a step between me and death. Then said Jonathan unto David, Whatsoever thy soul desireth, I will even do it for thee."

At their last meeting, Jonathan encouraged David. First Samuel 23:16 says: "And Jonathan Saul's son arose, and went to David into the wood, and strengthened his hand in God." David remembered Jonathan, for after Jonathan was killed and David became king, he took care of Mephibosheth, Jonathan's crippled son. Meeting a friend's need is the key to lasting friendships. Whatever the cost, meet those needs.

Shared secrets

King Saul's repeated attempts to take David's life kept David always looking over his shoulder. The closeness of David and Jonathan's friendship let them share their thoughts, and so they planned secretly to save David from Saul.

As David hid in the field near the palace of Saul, Jonathan signaled David that if it was safe he would shoot arrows beyond David. First Samuel 20:36, 39 says: "And he said unto his lad, Run, find out now the arrows which I shoot. And as the lad ran, he shot an arrow beyond him...But the lad knew not any thing: only Jonathan and David knew the matter."

David was reunited with his friend for a very brief period. First Samuel 20:41–42 says, "And as soon as the lad was gone, David arose out of a place toward the south, and fell on his face to the ground, and bowed himself three times: and they kissed one another, and wept one with another, until David exceeded. And Jonathan said to David, Go in peace, forasmuch as we have sworn both of us in the name of the LORD, saying, The LORD be between me and thee, and between my seed and thy seed for ever. And he arose and departed: and Jonathan went into the city."

These two had complete trust in each other as they shared their secrets. I'm so glad that my friend, the Lord Jesus, shares His innermost secrets with me. Remember John 15:15, "Henceforth I call you not servants; for the servant knoweth not what his lord doeth: but I have called you friends; for all things that I have heard of my Father I have made known unto you."

Real friends communicate honestly with each other; conflicts are worked out, and the friendship endures. Make it your goal to be a good friend. Remember, what you are as a friend is what you will get as a friend.

Rosalie Carter wrote:

> I think that God will never send
> A gift so precious as a friend.
> A friend who always understands
> And fills each need as it demands.
> Whose loyalty will stand the test
> When skies are bright or overcast.
> Who sees the faults that merit blame
> But keeps on loving just the same.
> Who does far more than creed could do
> To make us good, to make us true.
> Earth's gifts a sweet contentment lend,
> But only God can give a friend.

SUMMARY OF THIS CHAPTER

This chapter reveals a variety of friendships and the principles needed to retain true friends.

   I. The Kinds of Friendships
- A. The forgiving friend
- B. The fulfilling friend
- C. The fickle friend
- D. The flawed friend

  II. The Keys to Friendship
- A. Similar interests
- B. Sacrificial giving
- C. Steadfast loyalty
- D. Strengthening influence
- E. Sensitivity to needs
- F. Shared secrets

ACTION STEPS

Here are three action steps you can take to help you develop and strengthen your friendships with others. (Initial and date when completed.)

1. List on a 3x5 card the names of those you would consider to be true friends as we have seen in this chapter.

Initial _____ Date _____

2. Take time to contact all of your friends listed on the 3x5 card by phone, card, or e-mail, and thank them for being a friend.

   Initial _____ Date _____

3. List some ways in which you have been less than a good friend, and pray that the Lord will help you do better.

   Initial _____ Date _____

CHAPTER TEN

The Man's Wealth

It is a solemn truth that, with the money men get and the money
men spend, they either get closer to God or further from Him.

M oney immediately draws the attention of most people.
I remember being raised as a young boy in a relatively
poor home where money was prized—whether found in
a birthday card, a Christmas card, or from the "tooth fairy." I recall
one day walking along the road to get something from the store for
my Mom, and I spotted a $10 bill on the ground. It seemed like a
million dollars to a child in 1949. After that occurrence, I walked
with my head down, hoping to find other money on the ground.

In a sense, money is life because we spend most of our lives
working to make money. Money touches every facet of our lives
because we use it on rent, utilities, and food, and even though we
do not consciously think about it, we spend it automatically. So
money is a very big part of all of our lives. Money in and of itself
is neutral. It is neither good nor bad. However, depending on how
it is used, it can become good or bad. Thus, the use of money is

vitally important. We often misunderstand money and its use, but God has a wealth of information in His Word on this subject.

What does money mean to you? Success and happiness? The more you have, the better your life? Right? Wrong!

In 1923, nine of the world's most "successful" financiers met in Chicago's Edgewater Beach Hotel. To an outsider, they had everything any man could want—money, high position, fame and power. This group included:

> Charles M. Schwab, the president of the largest steel company
> Samuel Insull, the president of the largest electric
>   utility company
> Howard Hopson, the president of the largest gas company
> Arthur Cutten, the greatest wheat speculator
> Richard Whitney, the president of the New York
>   Stock Exchange
> Albert Fall, the Secretary of Interior in President
>   Harding's Cabinet
> Jesse Livermore, the greatest "bear" on Wall Street
> Ivar Kreuger, head of the world's greatest monopoly, Kreuger
>   & Toll Byggnads AB
> Leon Fraser, president of the Bank of International Settlements

But were these men truly successful and happy? They were very successful in making money, but not in living a meaningful life. Within twenty-five years each man had reaped what he had sown.

> Charles M. Schwab was forced into bankruptcy and lived the
>   last five years before his death on borrowed money.
> Samuel Insull not only died in a foreign land, a fugitive from
>   justice, but was penniless.
> Howard Hopson became insane.
> Arthur Cutten became insolvent and died abroad.
> Richard Whitney was convicted of embezzlement and sent
>   to prison.
> Albert Fall was pardoned from prison so he could die at
>   home—broke.

Jesse Livermore, Ivar Kreuger, and Leon Fraser each committed suicide.

Each man knew how to make a living, but none had learned how to live. Solomon realized the folly of wealth when he wrote, "He that loveth silver shall not be satisfied with silver; nor he that loveth abundance with increase: this is also vanity. When goods increase, they are increased that eat them: and what good is there to the owners thereof, saving the beholding of them with their eyes? The sleep of a labouring man is sweet, whether he eat little or much: but the abundance of the rich will not suffer him to sleep. There is a sore evil which I have seen under the sun, namely, riches kept for the owners thereof to their hurt. But those riches perish by evil travail: and he begetteth a son, and there is nothing in his hand. As he came forth of his mother's womb, naked shall he return to go as he came, and shall take nothing of his labour, which he may carry away in his hand. And this also is a sore evil, that in all points as he came, so shall he go: and what profit hath he that hath laboured for the wind? All his days also, he eateth in darkness, and he hath much sorrow and wrath with his sickness" (Ecclesiastes 5:10–17).

Equating "riches" with success and happiness are only two of the many distorted views towards money. Many Christian men struggle with some basic misconceptions on the subject of money. Here are just a few:

Poverty equates with spirituality.

God never impoverishes anyone because of his spirituality. Multitudes of those who are extremely poor around the world are godly believers. However, scores of those in poverty are ungodly. There is no necessary relationship between the two.

Money brings happiness.

How often have you even thought, "If I had a million dollars, all my cares would be gone and I would be happy"? But here are nine wealthy men who obviously did not find real happiness. According to 1 Timothy 6:10, often those with wealth have "pierced themselves through with many sorrows."

To be wealthy is a sin.

This is wrong because many godly men were very wealthy, as were Abraham and Job.

Money is the root of all evil.

As we already stated, money is neutral, and is neither good nor evil; it is the *love* of money that is the root of all evil according to 1 Timothy 6:10.

The Lord Jesus gives to us a parable regarding a master who gave out talents to his servants. A talent was a very large amount of money, not an ability. While the central point of the parable concerns the Lord's return, it also gives basic principles about money.

Matthew 25:14–15 states, "For the kingdom of heaven is as a man travelling into a far country, who called his own servants, and delivered unto them his goods. And unto one he gave five talents, to another two, and to another one; to every man according to his several ability; and straightway took his journey." The three servants handle the talents differently, and show us how the Lord views our use of the money He gives us.

> The Master gave to each servant according to his ability.
> The Master owns the talents and expects the servant to multiply what the Master has given him.
> Every servant must answer to the Master for his handling of the trust.
> The Master has the right to take away talents as it pleases Him.
> A servant is not judged by the number of talents he was given, but by how he used them.

So everything about these talents has to do with our attitude—not our aptitude. Money brings both blessings and perils, but God will never use money against a man.

The Perils of Wealth

Money can worry a man.

If you find yourself worried about money, then God is not controlling your life. If we operate according to His plan, God promises to meet our needs. Philippians 4:19 says, "But my God shall supply all your need according to his riches in glory by Christ Jesus."

We need not worry because Jesus tells us in Matthew 6:31, "Therefore take no thought, saying, What shall we eat? or, What shall we drink? or, Wherewithal shall we be clothed?" So do not worry about what you eat, drink, wear, or where you live, but keep your focus on the kingdom. Matthew 6:33 says, "But seek ye first the kingdom of God, and his righteousness; and all these things shall be added unto you."

Money can corrupt a man.

God never gives a man wealth to corrupt him. But when we take control, corruption comes. It begins with choices such as "I just got a good promotion with a big raise, and we have to move to another area where there is no good church," or "My new job requires me to leave my family extended periods of time, but they will be fine," or "Pastor, I can no longer serve my church because I have taken a second job to get ahead financially." In my forty years of ministry, I have seen that choices like these have moved many families away from the Lord and led to corruption.

Money can inflate a man's ego.

Men struggle with pride, and money can be a trap to feed a man's ego. James 2:1–4 talks about the natural tendency to favor a man with money. In Proverbs 6:16, God begins His "hate list," and right at the top is "a proud look." God help us to walk humbly before all, ignoring financial gain. Always give God the glory. Success in our eyes is not the same as success in God's eyes.

Money can create a hoarder.

There is a distinct difference between saving and hoarding. Jesus speaks about a rich fool in Luke 12:18–20 which says, "And he said, This will I do: I will pull down my barns, and build greater; and there will I bestow all my fruits and my goods. And I will say to my soul, Soul, thou hast much goods laid up for many years; take thine ease, eat, drink, and be merry. But God said unto him, Thou fool, this night thy soul shall be required of thee: then whose shall those things be, which thou hast provided?" Here was a man who heaped up goods for himself, and the Lord called him a fool.

We receive to be God's conduit to others. Jesus taught in Matthew 6:19, "Lay not up for yourselves treasures upon earth, where moth and rust doth corrupt, and where thieves break through and steal." We are not to hoard. We receive to give the Lord His portion, to take care of our families' needs, and to minister to others. Someone asked John D. Rockefeller's attorney how much he left behind when he died. "He left it all."

Money can stir a man's fleshly lusts.

Every man has to deal with carnal desires. The flesh wants to be coddled and have its desires met. We must be careful to maintain a spiritual perspective. "Comfort" and "things" are acceptable if they are in God's will for our lives. We must live as Paul stated in Philippians 4:11, "Not that I speak in respect of want: for I have learned, in whatsoever state I am, therewith to be content." We must learn to be content. Our spiritual condition is not based on poverty or on wealth, but on allowing God to be in control of our finances and on being content.

Money can bring a man into bondage.

There are scores of men in prison today because they have violated the law. There are, likewise, many men who have violated God's law and so find themselves in bondage.

Years ago if a man incurred and owed a debt that he would not or could not pay, he was sent to "debtors' prison" until the debt was paid. Mental bondage can be even worse than a debtors' prison. Most divorces and many suicides come about because of financial troubles. The following behaviors often lead to bondage:

Overdue bills. Eighty percent of Christian families suffer from over-spending, but Proverbs 27:12 says, "A prudent man foreseeth the evil, and hideth himself; but the simple pass on, and are punished."

Investment worries. Often investments cause great bondage as Matthew 6:24 says, "No man can serve two masters: for either he will hate the one, and love the other; or else he will hold to the one, and despise the other. Ye cannot serve God and mammon."

Get-rich-quick schemes. Many men are always looking for that easy money, but Proverbs 28:20 says, "…but he that maketh haste to be rich shall not be innocent."

No gainful employment. Some men are too lazy to work or find a job, while others cannot find gainful employment through no fault of their own. Second Thessalonians 3:10 says, "For even when we were with you, this we commanded you, that if any would not work, neither should he eat."

Deceitfulness. Some are dishonest in their financial dealings with others, but Romans 12:11 says, "Not slothful in business…."

Greediness. We want luxury, or more than we really need. First Timothy 6:6 says, "But godliness with contentment is great gain."

Covetousness. We look at others around us that have more than we do and want what they have. James 4:3 says, "Ye ask, and receive not, because ye ask amiss, that ye may consume it upon your lusts."

Over-commitment to work. We have over-commitment to a job or business and are failing to provide our families the time and nurture that they need. First Timothy 5:8 says, "But if any provide not for his own, and specially for those of his own house, he hath denied the faith, and is worse than an infidel."

No commitment to the Lord's work. We do not give the Lord what is rightfully His. Proverbs 3:9 says, "Honour the Lord with thy substance, and with the firstfruits of all thine increase."

Superiority. A man might look down on those with less, and doing so is sinful. Philippians 2:3 says, "Let nothing be done through strife or vainglory; but in lowliness of mind let each esteem other better than themselves."

We've seen the perils that can be attached to wealth. Now we will see what the Bible says about using wealth correctly.

The Principles of Wealth

In 1 Chronicles 29:10–14, David offers a great prayer of thanksgiving as he and all the people gave willingly to the task of building the temple. "Wherefore David blessed the Lord before all the congregation: and David said, Blessed be thou, Lord God of Israel our father, for ever and ever. Thine, O Lord, is the greatness, and the power, and the glory, and the victory, and the majesty: for all that is in the heaven and in the earth is thine; thine is the kingdom, O Lord, and thou art exalted as head above all. Both riches and honour come of thee, and thou reignest over all; and in thine hand is power and might; and in thine hand it is to make great, and to give strength unto all. Now therefore, our God, we thank thee, and praise thy glorious name. But who am I, and what is my people, that we should be able to offer so willingly after this sort? for all things come of thee, and of thine own have we given thee."

Someone has humorously said, "My money talks; its voice is strong, loud, and clear. It says, 'So long.'" Money comes and will always depart quickly. We must understand that money belongs to the Lord, and we are only its stewards.

Years ago, Dr. George W. Truett said that *all* that we possess "belongs to God." A wealthy rancher asked Dr. Truett out to his ranch the next day. As they strolled about the ranch where thousands of cattle grazed, the rancher spoke, "Until last night I looked upon these vast and valuable acres and these cattle as my own. Will you pray with me as I pray in my heart 'I give all that I have to God to be used as He directs'?" As Dr. Truett prayed, the rancher cried out to God, pleading, "Oh Lord, Oh God, Oh God, save him now. I give you my son."

That next Sunday as Dr. Truett was preaching, a young man stood to his feet and spoke, "Dr. Truett, preacher, I must trust Christ as my Saviour right now. I need and ask for His mercy and forgiveness." Dr. Truett could not finish his message as not only did the rancher's son come to be saved, but scores of others came as well. The Holy Spirit took charge of the service, revival broke out, and in the weeks following, hundreds were saved and scores got right with God.

The floodgates of great spiritual blessings will never be opened to us if we refuse to let possessions and people go and give God what rightfully belongs to Him. Jesus refers to wealth and possessions 288 times in His Word. In Matthew 6:21 He states, "For where your treasure is, there will your heart be also." Someone has said that you can tell a lot about a man's spiritual character by looking at his checkbook or his credit card account.

The young, rich ruler came to Christ, but he let his real estate stand between him and eternal life. The rich, barn-building fool bartered his soul for a few stalls full of hay. The rich man dined sumptuously and selfishly while the beggar, Lazarus, starved to death at his gate. He will have the eternal torments of hell to remember how he misused his money. Your attitude about money and wealth will reveal your attitude about God, His Word, His work and eternal life.

Recognize these three important biblical principles.

Principle of ownership

First, if you are saved, you belong to God. As 1 Peter 1:18–19 says, "Forasmuch as ye know that ye were not redeemed with corruptible things, as silver and gold, from your vain conversation received by tradition from your fathers; But with the precious blood of Christ, as of a lamb without blemish and without spot."

We now are the property of the Lord. According to 1 Corinthians 6:19–20: "What? know ye not that your body is the temple of the Holy Ghost which is in you, which ye have of God, and ye are not your own? For ye are bought with a price: therefore glorify God in your body, and in your spirit, which are God's."

You may say that nobody owns you. But, if you are born again, you belong to God; He owns you, and He has every right to what He owns. And so we and everything we possess belong to the Lord. Everything in this world belongs to God because He created all things. Every bar of gold, every gold coin, gold chain, or nugget of gold is His. All the silver, oil, diamonds and every precious stone are His as Haggai 2:8 says, "The silver is mine, and the gold is mine, saith the Lord of hosts." Everything we have and possess has been entrusted to us by God, and everything, therefore, is His.

First Corinthians 4:7 says, "For who maketh thee to differ from another? and what hast thou that thou didst not receive? now if thou didst receive it, why dost thou glory, as if thou hadst not received it?" When we understand these ideas then we can clearly see the next two principles.

Principle of stewardship

Stewardship deals with our response to God being the owner and us being the stewards or managers. First Corinthians 4:2 says, "Moreover it is required in stewards, that a man be found faithful." As a man honors his Saviour, the tithe is only the beginning of his stewardship. Proverbs 3:9 says, "Honour the Lord with thy substance, and with the firstfruits of all thine increase." According to Leviticus 27:30, "And all the tithe of the land, whether of the seed of the land, or of the fruit of the tree, is the LORD's: it is holy unto the LORD."

Tithing began before the law was given, because both Abraham and Jacob tithed as God blessed them. Jesus also endorsed the tithe. Failing to give back the tithe to our Lord is stealing from God. As Malachi 3:8 says, "Will a man rob God? Yet ye have robbed me. But ye say, Wherein have we robbed thee? In tithes and offerings."

OUR GIVING SHOULD BE PERIODIC.

According to 1 Corinthians 16:2: "Upon the first day of the week let every one of you lay by him in store, as God hath prospered him, that there be no gatherings when I come." Our giving is based on God's command, not on our emotions.

OUR GIVING SHOULD BE PERSONAL.

According to 1 Corinthians 16:2, "...let every one of you..." and in 2 Corinthians 9:7, "Every man according as he purposeth in his heart, so let him give; not grudgingly, or of necessity: for God loveth a cheerful giver." No one is exempt from stewardship. Everyone must do his part.

OUR GIVING SHOULD BE PROPORTIONATE.

When God gives us more, we can give more. Many men of great wealth were blessed because they gave generously (Mr. Colgate, Mr. Hershey, Mr. Latourneau, Mr. Rockefeller, to name a few). Second Corinthians 9:6, "But this I say, He which soweth sparingly shall reap also sparingly; and he which soweth bountifully shall reap also bountifully."

Principle of fellowship with God

We show that we love the things our Lord loves when we faithfully give to the Lord's work and thereby lay up treasure in Heaven. Matthew 6:20–21, "But lay up for yourselves treasures in heaven, where neither moth nor rust doth corrupt, and where thieves do not break through nor steal: For where your treasure is, there will your heart be also."

In the days of Hezekiah and Nehemiah, revival took place and was marked with the return of tithing because where there is no tithing, there is no revival. Dr. W. P. Walters states, "If a Christian is not right with God financially, he is not right with God period." Our real relationship with God is often revealed by our pattern of giving.

The Purposes of Wealth

In my garage I have an assortment of tools that can be used in a variety of ways. For example, a hammer can be used to pound a nail, pull a nail, straighten a nail, or find a stud in the wall. In the same way, God uses wealth as a tool for many purposes in our lives.

To develop our trustworthiness

Our personal finances say much about our relationship with the Lord. Can the Lord trust us? Luke 16:11, "If therefore ye have not been faithful in the unrighteous mammon, who will commit to your trust the true riches?"

To increase our trust in God

Do you have confidence in God as a faithful provider? Matthew 7:7–8, "Ask, and it shall be given you; seek, and ye shall find; knock, and it shall be opened unto you: For every one that asketh receiveth; and he that seeketh findeth; and to him that knocketh it shall be opened."

To reveal His love for us

As His children, we learn that our Heavenly Father loves and cares for us. Matthew 7:11, "If ye then being evil, know how to give good gifts unto your children, how much more shall your Father which is in heaven give good things to them that ask him?"

To show His mighty power

Our powerful provider delights to "…shew himself strong in the behalf of them whose heart is perfect toward him" (2 Chronicles 16:9). Jeremiah said it well in chapter 33:3: "Call unto me, and I will answer thee, and shew thee great and mighty things, which thou knowest not."

To unify God's people in His cause

God's people have always cared for one another. Acts 4:32 says, "And the multitude of them that believed were of one heart and of one soul: neither said any of them that ought of the things which he possessed was his own; but they had all things common."

To satisfy the needs of God's work

God's plan is for all to tithe to the local church. Malachi 3:10, "Bring ye all the tithes into the storehouse, that there may be meat in mine house, and prove me now herewith, saith the Lord of hosts, if I will not open you the windows of heaven, and pour you out a blessing, that there shall not be room enough to receive it."

The Planning of Wealth

We need to plan wisely to make preparation for the future as Proverbs 6:6–8 states, "Go to the ant, thou sluggard; consider her ways, and be wise: Which having no guide, overseer, or ruler, Provideth her meat in the summer, and gathereth her food in the harvest." We need to plan wisely, assess our finances, but always allow the Lord to lead us. Proverbs 16:1 says, "The preparations of the heart in man, and the answer of the tongue, is from the LORD."

Have short-range plans.

Wise short-range planning is a must for financial success.

Establish a budget. Establish a written plan listing your income and expenses to make sure you live within your means.

Commit to tithing. The first item in your budget should be your tithe. Offerings should be next.

Reduce or eliminate credit. Thousands of God's people suffer because they do not control credit card spending.

Seek godly counsel.

Have long-range goals.

Even as Joseph, by God's divine direction, gave Pharaoh plans for the ensuing famine, so we should make long-term plans.

Save on a regular basis. Establish a cushion for emergencies that will arise. Invest for your future with savings as well as stocks, bonds, real estate, etc. Be sure to get expert advice, and use wisdom.

Protect with insurance. Include both life and health insurance. Get unbiased advice—an agent is not unbiased.

Make out a will or a living trust. Get unbiased advice as to what would be best for your family's situation. Update it regularly as your situation changes.

SUMMARY OF THIS CHAPTER

We have covered vital areas regarding a man's wealth and given biblical direction so that the Lord can bless and use you.

    I.   The Perils of Wealth
   II.   The Principles of Wealth
  III.   The Purposes of Wealth
  IV.   The Planning of Wealth

ACTION STEPS

Here are three action steps you can take to handle more efficiently the wealth God gives you. (Initial and date when completed.)

1. Write out on a 3x5 card Matthew 6:19–21, and memorize it.

   Initial _____ Date _____

2. Find your financial giving report from your church, and determine what percentage you have given specifically to the Lord in general giving, missions, building fund and other.

   Initial _____ Date _____

3. Look at your present budget or write out a monthly budget, and evaluate whether or not you are operating in a balanced and biblical manner.

   Initial _____ Date _____

CHAPTER ELEVEN

The Man's Wife

A godly and obedient husband will greatly
reduce or eliminate most marriage problems.

Aman's relationship with his wife is very challenging. Most husbands, if they were totally frank, would admit that their marriage is not what it should be. Unfortunately, most men do not wake up and change until they meet a major marital problem.

The story is told of an ocean liner that many years ago was crossing the Atlantic when suddenly a severe storm developed. It became so severe that suddenly one woman lost her footing and was swept overboard. As the passengers watched with horror, a man dove into the icy water.

He grabbed the floundering woman and held onto her until a lifeboat was lowered to rescue them. When they arrived on deck, the people were astonished and embarrassed to see that the rescuer was the oldest man on ship—in his eighties! When called on to make a short speech at the celebratory dinner held that night, the old man rose slowly, looked around and said, "I have just one question to ask. Who pushed me?"

Quite often men need a push to change their marriage for the better. Many have the attitude that "I'm okay, and my marriage is fine." But their marriage may lack love. We men must lead to have the right kind of marriage and family.

Most of us can be quite self-centered; we love ourselves first. But God says to love Him first. Matthew 22:37–38 says, "Jesus said unto him, Thou shalt love the Lord thy God with all thy heart, and with all thy soul, and with all thy mind. This is the first and great commandment." And then we are to love our wives even as "…Christ also loved the church, and gave himself for it;" (Ephesians 5:25).

The old saying goes "that marriages are made in Heaven, but maintenance occurs on earth." We need to continually maintain our marriages because our wives have needs. Some wives are "low maintenance." Other wives require "high maintenance." However, all wives need some maintenance.

Every man who has a car or truck that he really loves, wants it to last a long time. He keeps that vehicle well maintained and clean so that he can continue to enjoy it. If we want to truly enjoy our wives, we have to work and perform regular maintenance. We must truly understand what real love is. John 15:13 says, "Greater love hath no man than this, that a man lay down his life for his friends."

Valentine's Day has become a "national holiday" to express love to our families, sweethearts, and friends by sending a card (to friends) or gifts (to sweethearts and family). While we honor our spouses on this day, we must remember that it is good to show love all days, not just occasionally. Remember that "first love" you had for your spouse?

Peter speaks about the relationship with our wives in 1 Peter 3:7: "Likewise, ye husbands, dwell with them according to knowledge, giving honour unto the wife, as unto the weaker vessel, and as being heirs together of the grace of life; that your prayers be not hindered." God's Word instructs us to:

Live with your wife.

We are to "dwell with them" which means to be closely united in a tight relationship. Show your love to the one you cherish by giving her attention.

Know your wife.

"...dwell with them according to knowledge...." Know her deep fears and cares, and her disappointments or expectations, and her scars and secrets. Be sensitive and be willing to listen. Become involved in her needs. Talk to her.

Honor your wife.

We must give "honour to the wife, as unto the weaker vessel." We must make our wives the "queen" of our lives, and see them as precious treasures. The word *honor* is synonymous with the word *precious* which is found in 1 Peter 1:19: "But with the precious blood of Christ, as of a lamb without blemish and without spot." Wives are truly precious treasures, so take care of yours! Show honor by telling her she is precious, by protecting her and treating her like a queen.

Continued praise is needed even for everyday tasks such as doing the dishes, making the bed, or running the vacuum. Proverbs 31 gives us twenty-one characteristics of a woman who deserves her husband's praise. Let's praise our wives.

We tend to assume our wives know how much they mean to us, and we think they have the ability to read our minds. They don't! Assume nothing! Tell her you love her and show her your love.

Wives are to be considered weaker vessels, not inferior vessels. God designed a woman to be different from a man in a variety of ways. Over the years I have witnessed these differences in my own home and ministry. The following is not original with me, but is a compilation from the materials I have studied. We need to learn to understand our wives.

A Wife's Diverse Struggles

A wife needs acceptance.

Your wife needs to feel her husband views her as a person of worth. She needs to be told that she is of worth very frequently. Many women fear they are rejected, even if they are not.

A wife needs assurance.

The husband needs to reassure his wife over and over of his love and her worth.

A wife needs her own identity.

She is often asking the question, "Who am I? Will someone please tell me who I am?" Loss of identity is a common problem for a wife. A sudden change of location or events may cause an identity crisis. As a mother brings up her children, she pours her life into them, and then they grow up and leave. The empty nest can cause an identity challenge. She must see herself as an individual, not just someone's wife or someone's mother. Otherwise if her husband dies and her children leave she will have no identity in her own mind.

A wife needs backing and support.

She needs to feel that her husband is on her side even when he may not completely agree with her ideas or actions. A wife is shattered when she feels that her husband is not in her corner.

A wife needs understanding.

A wife needs to feel understood. Certainly, while we can never totally understand one another, if we make a sustained effort to try, we will do better than if we do nothing.

A wife needs trust.

Nothing is more debilitating to a wife than for her husband to distrust her. When you have faith in her, you say, "I look upon you as a trustworthy person."

A wife needs her husband's confidence.

Confidence is more than trust. She bases her value as a person on her husband's valuation of her various abilities. She must feel that he thinks her to be competent and able.

A wife needs attention.

She needs to feel that she is on her husband's mind. The little things you do for her, such as opening the door for her or seating her at the table give positive or negative clues as to her husband's care.

A wife needs praises.

She needs praise for completing everyday tasks as well as for understanding Scripture. She does not divide her life into compartments, and so a failure or a praise in one area spreads to the others.

A wife needs rest and "time off."

The old saying "a woman's work is never done" expresses a good wife's sense of responsibility. She will drive herself to total exhaustion if not encouraged to rest. Don't be a "slave driver."

A wife needs leadership.

If she is not led, independence and frustration will be the result. If you want her to follow, you must lead, plan, and give devotion to her.

A wife needs tender, loving care.

There will be times when only TLC will work. "Just hold me," will often be her plea. The wise husband should not need further explanation.

A wife needs to voice her opinions.

If she doesn't feel you are seriously listening to her she will feel rejected. A wise husband will listen and consider her thoughts and insights. You might occasionally take her suggestions; otherwise she may feel you are only paying lip service to her thoughts.

A wife needs protection for her welfare.

You need to help her set physical and spiritual boundaries. A good husband is responsible to protect his wife, even from herself and a desire to do too much in any area.

A wife needs to be included in financial matters.

Many wives have the capability to assist in finances. She needs freedom to spend money "as her own" with measured limitations. She also needs to know all aspects of family finances. You do not know when you will be called home. Grieving is hard enough, but a woman who is kept in the dark finds herself totally at a loss when suddenly she has to make all decisions alone and knows absolutely nothing. Protect your wife.

A wife needs pretty things.

The aesthetic sense of a woman is a gift from God. Every woman delights to receive beautiful things. It would be a dull world without our wives' tastes.

A wife needs attention to her medical needs.

When she is sick, she needs your care, sympathy, and support more than at any other time. Give her the medication she needs and take her to her appointments. She will appreciate you greatly.

Now that you know your wife's needs, how do you intend to meet them? Husbands are commanded to take responsibility to lead their families. Ephesians 5:23 and 25 says, "For the husband is the head of the wife, even as Christ is the head of the church: and he is the saviour of the body…Husbands, love your wives, even as Christ also loved the church, and gave himself for it." We are to love our wives in a Christ-like, sacrificial, "agape" love. Just as a politician serves his constituency, a pastor his congregation, a physician his patients, and a proprietor his customers; a husband serves his wife. Consider the following:

A Husband's Dedicated Solutions

Be a spiritual leader.

Leadership is judged by whether or not a man grows in his relationship with God (i.e., the direction his life is taking). Wives do not expect perfection, just progress in the right direction.

Wives struggle to follow dictatorial demands, but when there is a loving example, this is a great motivation for a wife to follow. Ephesians 4:32, "And be ye kind one to another, tenderhearted, forgiving one another, even as God for Christ's sake hath forgiven you." Colossians 3:14, "And above all these things put on charity, which is the bond of perfectness."

A DESIRE TO FOLLOW GOD

Colossians 3:1–2, "If ye then be risen with Christ, seek those things which are above, where Christ sitteth on the right hand of God. Set your affection on things above, not on things on the earth." Your wife needs to know that you delight in the Lord and seek Him. Spiritual maturity comes by a consistent, growing relationship with your Lord.

CONVICTIONS BASED UPON THE WORD

As your wife sees you reading your Bible, giving to the Lord, attending church regularly, being a consistent soulwinner, and living out the Word, she will follow your leadership and set similar standards for her own life.

COMMITMENT TO FOLLOW CONVICTIONS
By obedience to biblical standards, you show your wife that she must do the same. It is not what you say, but what you do that will influence your wife.

Be a special man.

Every wife needs to often hear those three little words, "I love you." I heard of a young husband who was asked by his young wife, "Tell me those three little words that make me feel lightheaded and like I'm walking on air." He stupidly replied, "Go hang yourself."

Telling your wife that you love her or that she is special is important, but it is not enough. She wants you to show her that she is special and that she meets your needs. God made your wife to be a help meet (e.g., a suitable helper) for you. Genesis 2:18, "And the LORD God said, It is not good that the man should be alone; I will make him an help meet for him." Your wife is the completer to make you whole.

My wife helps me and challenges me in many ways. She makes my life truly fulfilled. Let your wife know how much you need her and that she is uniquely special to you. The most devastating action of a husband is to give another woman a task that should be done only by his wife. To praise the other woman for doing that task adds insult to injury. You are there to make your spouse feel special, and one of her great needs is to feel needed. Let your wife know what she can do to help you and then praise her for her help.

Be a sensitive husband.

Your wife needs to know and hear you rehearse the character qualities, personality traits, and family qualities that attracted you to her. She needs to be reminded of how wonderful and special she is to you and why she is special.

Every wife has some measure of struggle with insecurity, and the growing proof that you cherish your wife is your ability to take unchangeable physical features and personality characteristics which she has trouble accepting and praising them. Wives are often sensitive about their physical features, so compliment and encourage her in positive ways. The glow and radiance of a wife is usually a reflection of a loving and sensitive husband.

Be a safety inspector.

As we briefly mentioned earlier, every wife has a great need to be understood, so become a student of your wife. Husbands need to know the boundaries of their spouse. A wife wants her husband to be aware of her strengths and weaknesses and to have the wisdom to provide a loving, firm direction so that she will not fail by going beyond her limitations.

Occasionally your wife will ask you for something she really doesn't want. She is testing you to see if you are perceptive to her dangers. If you give her what she wants, she will become insecure. Your priority is to understand your wife the best you can, to know when to be firm and when to be lenient. Always be sensitive and keep a loving spirit.

Be a sharing mate.

A wife needs to know her husband enjoys spending time with her in intimate conversation, which is only possible when there is oneness of spirit. If she cannot have this with you she will find it through someone else. A wife has many things to tell her husband, and a wise husband will become a good listener. If she senses you are "tuned out" or in a hurry or preoccupied, she won't really open up to tell what she really feels. Make sure you communicate with the right tone of voice and body language, as most wives are extremely sensitive to both.

Remember that when you married your wife, you relinquished the full rights of yourself to your wife. Ephesians 5:21 says, "Submitting yourselves one to another in the fear of God." Ephesians 5:31, "For this cause shall a man leave his father and mother, and shall be joined unto his wife, and two shall be one flesh." Half of her enjoyment is anticipating these times of communication. Schedule a date night on a regular basis and actually talk! Failure to communicate will result in a wife becoming bitter, fearful, and frustrated.

Be a supporting partner.

Become close to your wife. Genesis 2:24 says, "Therefore shall a man leave his father and his mother, and shall cleave unto his wife: and they shall be one flesh." We as husbands are to *cleave* to our wives, which means to stick to them like glue. We have become one flesh in our marriage union. You need to show your wife you notice her by talking to her and helping her in her work. You won her and her parents' approval by being attentive. Your wife remembers your former attentiveness and love, and now feels lonely and shut out if these are missing.

Your wife can measure your attention and care—these show how much she is a part of your life. You must constantly work on these actions. If you treat your wife like a queen one day and neglect her the next, she will feel insecure and fearful of being hurt, so be consistent.

In conclusion, God has given us some grave marital responsibilities. Review Ephesians 5:21–29 and Colossians 3:12–19 on a regular basis to remember how to be the husband God wants you to be. Note that the Ephesians passage commands us to be filled with the Holy Spirit before it deals with marriage relationships. Remember, you cannot be a good husband without the Holy Spirit's power and guidance. The more wisely you invest in your marriage, the greater the rewards.

SUMMARY OF THIS CHAPTER

This chapter is probably one of the most challenging, yet it will reap for you some of the greatest rewards in life. Make your marriage a little bit of heaven on earth.

    I. A Wife's Diverse Struggles
   II. A Husband's Dedicated Solutions

ACTION STEPS

Here are three action steps you can take to strengthen your marriage relationship. (Initial and date when completed.)

1. On a 3x5 card write out 1 Peter 3:7, and memorize it.

    Initial _____ Date _____

2. On a piece of paper write out the six dedicated solutions covered in this chapter. Review them regularly and put them to memory.

    Initial _____ Date _____

3. Make a list of at least five ways you can improve and strengthen your marriage, and tell these to your wife.

    Initial _____ Date _____

CHAPTER TWELVE

The Man's Wisdom

The greatest need for any man, as he traverses
through the maze of life, is not wealth, fame or
even health, but God's divine wisdom.

The direction of a man's life determines where he will end; so every step must be correct. There are always two choices before us. One choice is directed by heavenly wisdom from the Lord, and the other is drawn by earthly wisdom if a man chooses it. James 3:13–18 says, "Who is a wise man and endued with knowledge among you? let him shew out of a good conversation his works with meekness of wisdom. But if ye have bitter envying and strife in your hearts, glory not, and lie not against the truth. This wisdom descendeth not from above, but is earthly, sensual, devilish. For where envying and strife is, there is confusion and every evil work. But the wisdom that is from above is first pure, then peaceable, gentle, and easy to be intreated, full of mercy and good fruits, without partiality, and without hypocrisy. And the fruit of righteousness is sown in peace of them that make peace."

If you have ever been in a maze, you can identify with the fact that getting from point A to point B requires choices. Some choices are good. They help you get closer to your planned destination. However, others cause you to go in circles, backtrack or end in a cul-de-sac. You might think, "If only I could have an elevated platform to see the entire maze, then I could see where I should go to reach the end." I am glad that Jesus in His omniscience knows all from beginning to end, and that He tells me how to choose. So many men go on blindly, only hoping that they are going in the right direction. Often good men have wasted years or whole lives because they ignored God's direction and made wrong choices.

Every man needs God's wisdom daily because seemingly small choices either lead *to* our goal or *away* from it. James 1:5–8 says, "If any of you lack wisdom, let him ask of God, that giveth to all men liberally, and upbraideth not; and it shall be given him. But let him ask in faith, nothing wavering. For he that wavereth is like a wave of the sea driven with the wind and tossed. For let not that man think that he shall receive any thing of the Lord. A double minded man is unstable in all his ways."

Man is clever and has accomplished amazing feats in many fields. Man can travel higher, faster, and further than one could have ever imagined even just a few years ago. Yet man living without God's guidance makes no spiritual or moral progress. Like the man in the maze, he goes backward, in circles, to dead ends. Man thinks he is so smart and so creative, yet his life is empty and void until the Lord Jesus Christ takes control. Proverbs 14:12 says, "There is a way which seemeth right unto a man, but the end thereof are the ways of death."

I am so glad that in the "midnight times of life," with the most difficult of decisions, God's Word says in Isaiah 58:11, "And the LORD shall guide thee continually, and satisfy thy soul in drought, and make fat thy bones: and thou shalt be like a watered garden, and like a spring of water, whose waters fail not." When we face any decision, we must cry to the Lord, "Which way shall I go, and where should I turn?" And the reply comes back as Psalm 32:8 says, "I will instruct thee and teach thee in the way which thou shalt go: I will guide thee with mine eye." The Lord has already gone before us and prepared the way. As the old chorus says "My Lord knows the way through the wilderness, all I have to do is follow."

Regardless of our vocations, secular or sacred, we all need God's heavenly wisdom not found in secular books, university programs, or motivational speakers. God's wisdom is readily available to any born-again Christian. His wisdom does not require riches or college degrees, but is freely available to any man of any age.

Several years ago I received a special mailing from a local car dealership. Inside the mailing was a beautifully colored promotional ad featuring a large treasure chest with a wide-open lid and a brand new car extending out of the chest. At the bottom of the flier was a key fastened by a piece of tape, with the words "Your key could win you this new car." Of course I had to go down to the dealership to see if my key would be the one to open it. God offers to each man a treasure chest of great wisdom, and the key we have is "ask and believe." Consider these thoughts:

Resisting Is Man's Problem

There is one great roadblock to attaining God's wisdom—pride. Satan has been using pride as early as the Garden of Eden to cause man to fall. Pride touches every man's life to some degree; it makes men unproductive for God's use. No other sin will do more to dam the floodgates of revival, destroy homes, devastate lives, and drain the power of God's men than the pride which blinds us to its presence.

Self-acceptance is not pride.

Everyone who is saved is viewed as valuable in God's eyes. Ephesians 1:6–8 says, "To the praise of the glory of his grace, wherein he hath made us accepted in the beloved. In whom we have redemption through his blood, the forgiveness of sins, according to the riches of his grace; Wherein he hath abounded toward us in all wisdom and prudence." Understanding God's view of His children gives us confidence because we know we are loved and accepted.

Rejoicing in honor is not pride.

Honor means to esteem or regard highly, to merit, to respect. The Bible is filled with instruction to honor others as it says, "Give honor to whom honor is due." A man should properly honor his wife. We need to properly give and honor those in authority over us as they "watch for [our] souls."

Satisfaction of a job well done is not pride.

Colossians 3:23 says, "And whatsoever ye do, do it heartily, as to the Lord, and not unto men." You need to be diligent, committed to do everything as to the Lord. At work, at home, and at church, do your best and rejoice in your work.

Pride is feeling that you are independent of God. It includes ingratitude and self-centeredness. Here is a simple quiz to determine if you harbor pride.

1. Does it irritate you when someone corrects you for your faults?
2. When you make a mistake, do you always have an alibi?
3. When someone wrongs you, do you say, "I don't need him"?
4. Do you find it hard to ask for advice?
5. Do you find yourself ungrateful?
6. Do you measure success by victories over others?

Answering "yes" to any of these means you are proud.

Pride reviles Deity.

God says He hates pride. Proverbs 16:5 says, "Every one that is proud in heart is an abomination to the LORD." James 4:6 says, "…Wherefore he saith, God resisteth the proud, but giveth grace unto the humble." God hates pride because of what it does to us.

God gives a "hate list" in Proverbs 6:16–19: "These six things doth the LORD hate: yea, seven are an abomination unto him: A proud look, a lying tongue, and hands that shed innocent blood, An heart that deviseth wicked imaginations, feet that be swift in running to mischief, A false witness that speaketh lies, and he that soweth discord among brethren."

Pride caused the greatest and most beautiful of God's angels, Lucifer (meaning "light-bearer") to become the devil. Ezekiel says in chapter 28:15 that he was perfect in all his ways "…till iniquity was found" in him. His pride corrupted him. Isaiah 14:12–14 says, "How art thou fallen from heaven, O Lucifer, son of the morning! how art thou cut down to the ground, which didst weaken the nations! For thou hast said in thine heart, I will ascend into heaven, I will exalt my throne above the stars of God: I will sit also upon the mount of the congregation, in the sides of the north: I will ascend above the heights of the clouds: I will be like the most High."

The pride of man began in Eden and plunged the entire human race into its present sinful condition. Pride is an affront to a gracious God! Today, lost men often will not believe in Christ because of their independence and pride.

Pride reveals depravity.

Our pride and our wicked depravity make us act as if we do not need God constantly. How many days have we neglected personal time with God—reading His Word and looking to Him for direction in our lives? The opportunities for communion in prayer go by as we waste time pursuing our plans without consulting God. The hole in the apple is not created by a worm trying to get in, but by a worm on the inside trying to get out. That egg was laid on the blossom so that when the apple formed from the blossom, the egg was already inside. In the same way, we were born with an old Adamic nature, and so we are born with pride.

Pride revives disunity.

According to Proverbs 13:10, "Only by pride cometh contention...." There has never been a war or conflict not caused by pride. Every church-split, every argument, every marital disagreement, and every divorce are partially caused by pride.

It is our pride (or self-centeredness) that creates disunity in our homes. There are no problems too great to solve, only people too small to solve them. Matthew 12:25 states, "And Jesus knew their thoughts, and said unto them, Every kingdom divided against itself is brought to desolation; and every city or house divided against itself shall not stand."

Our conflicts with others would soon be resolved if we laid aside our pride, humbled ourselves, and lived a crucified life. You cannot fight a dead man; he will not react. Galatians 2:20 says, "I am crucified with Christ: nevertheless I live; yet not I, but Christ liveth in me: and the life which I now live in the flesh I live by the faith of the Son of God, who loved me, and gave himself for me." If we acted as if we were crucified (dead), we would not allow pride to ruin our relationships.

Pride brings destruction.

The Scriptures are filled with examples of tragedies caused by pride. As Proverbs 15:25 says, "The LORD will destroy the house of the proud...." And notice Proverbs 16:18: "Pride goeth before destruction, and an haughty spirit before a fall."

Look at these examples:

PRIDE PRODUCES NATIONAL RUIN.

Nations that turn against God will ultimately meet their end. What happened at the Tower of Babel and with Israel, God's chosen people, are two examples of the results of national pride. Today, America is running quickly to the same ruin. One only has to look at history to see the devastating results of a proud nation.

PRIDE PRODUCES DOMESTIC RUIN.

Pride has destroyed or damaged millions of homes. Pride causes dysfunctional families because men seek their own desires over the needs of their families.

PRIDE PRODUCES FINANCIAL RUIN.

Pride causes men to want to out-do others. Therefore, they over-spend and find themselves a slave to lenders. Men fail to learn the key to contentment and instead find themselves on a path to ruin.

PRIDE PRODUCES SPIRITUAL RUIN.

The Bible is replete with stories of people with great potential who were ruined by pride. For example, the proud and disobedient heart of Saul, the first king of Israel, led him to do "his thing" instead of following God's direct commands. Samuel promises God's condemnation in 1 Samuel 15:23, "For rebellion is as the sin of witchcraft, and stubbornness is as iniquity and idolatry. Because thou hast rejected the word of the LORD, he hath also rejected thee from being king."

Consider what Isaac Watts stated in this wonderful hymn: "When I survey the wondrous cross, on which the Prince of Glory died, my richest gain I count but loss and pour contempt on all my pride." If we can lay aside our sinful pride, we can let God's divine wisdom control us.

Receiving God's Provision

Solomon was unique because his wisdom exceeded that of man. He asked God in 1 Kings 3:7–9, "And now, O LORD my God, thou has made thy servant king instead of David my father: and I am but a little child: I know not how to go out or come in. And thy servant is in the midst of thy people which thou hast chosen, a great people, that cannot be numbered nor counted for multitude. Give therefore thy servant an understanding heart to judge thy people, that I may discern between good and bad: for who is able to judge this thy so great a people?"

Solomon's request pleased God, who said in 1 Kings 3:12: "Behold, I have done according to thy words: lo, I have given thee a wise and an understanding heart; so that there was none like thee before thee, neither after thee shall any arise like unto thee."

Shortly afterward, the Lord gave him opportunity to use his gift. First Kings 3:16–18 says that two prostitutes with one living baby and one dead baby were arguing whose baby the living child was. Solomon, in divine wisdom, ordered the living baby to be cut in half, and the real mother cried out, "No, No, give the other woman the baby," thus revealing that she was the baby's mother. First Kings 3:28 says: "And all Israel heard of the judgment which the king had judged; and they feared the king: for they saw that the wisdom of God was in him, to do judgment."

The book of Proverbs, by Solomon, is a great book of wisdom. Every person should read through this book monthly, a chapter a day. One simple passage gives a formula for receiving God's divine wisdom. Remember that wisdom comes by asking in faith.

The Bible is the source of all wisdom according to Deuteronomy 4:5–6: "Behold, I have taught you statutes and judgments, even as the LORD my God commanded me, that ye should do so in the land whither ye go to possess it. Keep therefore and do them; for this is your wisdom and your understanding in the sight of the nations, which shall hear all these statues, and say, Surely this great nation is a wise and understanding people."

Jesus Christ is called the source of all wisdom. Colossians 2:3 says, "In whom are hid all the treasures of wisdom and knowledge." The Holy Spirit is the giver of wisdom as Exodus 31:3 says, "And I have filled him with the spirit of God, in wisdom, and in understanding, and in knowledge, and in all manner of workmanship." And, finally Proverbs 3:5–6 says, "Trust in the LORD with all thine heart; and lean not unto thine own understanding. In all thy ways acknowledge him, and he shall direct thy paths." Proverbs 3:5–6 tells us to have:

A trusting confidence

"Trust in the Lord with all thine heart…." Trust is the only way to wisdom. Just as we trust in Jesus Christ as Saviour, we must trust Him for daily wisdom. Do not trust in your own ideas and fleshly wisdom. Proverbs 28:26 says, "He that trusteth in his own heart is a fool: but whoso walketh wisely, he shall be delivered."

Our trust in God is found in knowing Him, because we will not trust someone we do not know. John says we must abide in Christ (John 15:1–10 mentions *abide* nine times). *Abiding* speaks of a place of fellowship and communion with Christ. A deeper walk with the Lord will result in a deeper faith in our Saviour.

Proverbs 3:5 states "…and lean not unto thine own understanding." To have God's mind takes uncommon sense as Proverbs 3:7 states, "Be not wise in thine own eyes…." Simply stated, do not rely on your own ideas or desires. We sometimes say, "the Lord is leading me to do such and such," when what we are really doing is following our desires—not the Lord's.

Isaiah says in chapter 55:8–9: "For my thoughts are not your thoughts, neither are your ways my ways, saith the LORD. For as the heavens are higher than the earth, so are my ways higher than your ways, and my thoughts than your thoughts." We often scheme to follow our own will and thereby completely desert God's will.

A total commitment

The passage continues with "…in all thy ways acknowledge him…" demanding a whole-hearted decision to follow God's wisdom. I remember struggling with God's will for my life while sitting in a church service on a Sunday evening long ago while my pastor preached from Acts 10. In that passage Peter saw a great sheet lowered from heaven filled with all kinds of unclean animals. A voice from Heaven commanded Peter to "rise, kill and eat," but Peter, thinking of Jewish dietary laws said, "…Not so Lord." But how could he say, "Not so," and call his Saviour, "my Lord"?

That night was the turning point of my life. I decided in all my ways I must acknowledge the Lord first. The Lord has the right to direct us according to His good pleasure, not ours. Paul correctly pleaded in Romans 12:1: "I beseech you therefore, brethren, by the mercies of God, that ye present your bodies a living sacrifice, holy, acceptable unto God, which is your reasonable service."

The story is told of a brilliant, young man raised on the mission field in Africa who wanted to be an engineer. He went to one of the finest universities in England and graduated at the top of his class. He had wanted to make money, have fame and plenty of leisure time. But he became deathly sick and was taken to the hospital to be told he had only a short time to live.

A letter came from his father who had no idea of his son's condition. He closed his letter with these words, "Only one life twill soon be past, only what's done for Christ will last." In the stillness of his hospital room, the young man prayed and wrote in his diary. "Lord, anywhere, anytime, any cost, amen." You will never be happy unless you have God's wisdom and follow His direction. John 4:34 says, "Jesus saith unto them, My meat is to do the will of him that sent me, and to finish his work."

Notice that our job is to walk in wisdom by trusting in the Lord, refraining from our own understanding, and acknowledging Him in every area of our lives.

A thrilling consequence

"…he shall direct thy paths."

HE

It is God that directs our paths; we do not. God is all sufficient and gives us both direction and wisdom. He is omnipotent, omniscient, and omnipresent, ready to give us just what we need just when we need it. All the names of our God in the Bible give us so much insight of His capabilities. Notice that the name *Lord,* given many times over, is His name *Jehovah,* meaning the eternal self-existent one who delights to reveal Himself.

SHALL

It is not that He may or might, but that He will engage Himself with any child of God who wants to have His direction.

DIRECT

His wisdom may come as we read His Word in our devotions, when we hear the preaching or teaching of the Scriptures, or when praying. Other times, His will is revealed by His providence, that is, through circumstances as His leading is revealed.

Sometimes as the Holy Spirit helps us to renew, we sense God's direction. The Hebrew verb for *direct* is *yashur,* and simply means to cut a path or to clear the way. The Lord is our trailblazer, our pathfinder, who leads us in the path of true wisdom.

THY PATHS

Sometimes the path is smooth, but some of the paths that He chooses for us are rough, and we must cling and rely on Him completely. He is always by our side, ever ready to strengthen us. Psalm 37:23 says, "The steps of a good man are ordered by the LORD…." Our steps are literally prepared for us because He has blazed the trail ahead of us. God's will is not a roadmap, but a relationship.

In this journey through the maze of life, we need a direction finder, which comes from the wisdom we have as we walk hand-in-hand with our Lord.

SUMMARY OF THIS CHAPTER

This chapter shows the necessity of knowing and loving God by following His wisdom—not ours—in life.

    I. Resisting Is Man's Problem
        A. Pride reviles Deity.
        B. Pride reveals depravity.
        C. Pride revives disunity.
        D. Pride brings destruction.
   II. Receiving God's Provision
        A. A trusting confidence
        B. A total commitment
        C. A thrilling consequence

ACTION STEPS

Here are three action steps you can take to walk in wisdom throughout your life. (Initial and date when completed.)

1. Write out on a 3x5 card Proverbs 3:5–6 and put it to memory.

   Initial _____ Date _____

2. Consider the areas that your pride has hindered you from walking in wisdom. List those ways on a sheet of paper, and pray for victory in those areas.

   Initial _____ Date _____

3. Commit to reading through the book of Proverbs each month by reading a chapter a day.

   Initial _____ Date _____

PART THREE

The Completion in Becoming a Man of God

The completion of a man's life will reveal all that he is in reality without any area or part of the structure having been unveiled.

CHAPTER THIRTEEN

The Man's Wreath

*Every man will invest his life in something that will
ultimately be revealed and then either be destroyed or
rewarded at the Judgment Seat of Christ.*

M ost of our lives and energies focus on circumstances that
surround us, not on eternity that awaits us. Every area
of our lives and all of our decisions affect what happens
in eternity. Jesus warns us not to store up earthly treasures without
caring for eternity. In Matthew 6:19–21 Jesus says, "Lay not up for
yourselves treasures upon earth, where moth and rust doth corrupt,
and where thieves break through and steal: But lay up for yourselves
treasures in heaven, where neither moth nor rust doth corrupt,
and where thieves do not break through nor steal: For where your
treasure is, there will your heart be also."

While we are told to care for our families and our future here,
society pushes us to value material wealth over eternal values—a
great error. We will only truly understand life's meaning when we
stand before the Judgment Seat of Christ to be rewarded—or not.
"Only one life twill soon be past, only what's done for Christ will last"
may be old, but it is still true. Think carefully about the following:

The Realities We Live

When someone speaks of investments, we most often think of stocks, bonds, or property. While these have temporal value, only investment in God's kingdom has lasting value.

Time invested for Christ

Time is our most valuable commodity. And so we must never fritter away time instead of investing it in God's work. Time spent in Bible reading and prayer, or in study or on memorizing God's Word is worthwhile. There are innumerable ways to use our time. Choose worthwhile ones.

Colossians 3:1–2 says, "If ye then be risen with Christ, seek those things which are above, where Christ sitteth on the right hand of God. Set your affection on things above, not on things on the earth." Ephesians 5:15–17 says, "See then that ye walk circumspectly, not as fools, but as wise, Redeeming the time, because the days are evil. Wherefore be ye not unwise, but understanding what the will of the Lord is."

Service rendered for Christ

When we are saved, we receive spiritual gifts to be used in God's work in our lives. Paul says in 1 Corinthians 12:1, 11, "Now concerning spiritual gifts, brethren, I would not have you ignorant...But all these worketh that one and the selfsame Spirit, dividing to every man severally as he will." Ephesians 4:7 states, "But unto every one of us is given grace according to the measure of the gift of Christ." There are at least sixteen or more of these gifts listed in Scripture. (See my book, *Steps of a Good Man*, chapter 4.)

God saved us to serve Him by ministering to others for His glory, as well as for the good of others and ourselves. What are you doing as an important player in God's economy to serve the Lord through your local church? Your service ministers to others and helps you grow as a believer. Eternity will reveal all that was accomplished as you engaged in the Lord's work.

Children you have reared

You are to groom your children to carry the Lord's testimony worldwide. Psalm 127:3, "Lo, children are an heritage of the Lord and the fruit of the womb is his reward." Even though children make their own (sometimes poor) choices as they mature, and though they may disappoint us, we are to do our best to rear them correctly. Ephesians 6:4 says, "And, ye fathers, provoke not your children to wrath: but bring them up in the nurture and admonition of the Lord."

God instructed His people in Deuteronomy 6:5–9 beginning with the "Shema," and continuing with instructions for child-rearing: "And thou shat love the Lord thy God with all thine heart, and with all thy soul, and with all thy might. And these words, which I command thee this day, shall be in thine heart: And thou shalt teach them diligently unto thy children, and shalt talk of them when thou sittest in thine house, and when thou walkest by the way, and when thou liest down, and when thou risest up. And thou shalt bind them for a sign upon thine hand, and they shall be as frontlets between thine eyes. And thou shalt write them upon the posts of thy house, and on thy gates." Take time with your children as they are your investment for eternity.

Souls you have led to Christ

A great joy of the Christian man is to be an ambassador for Christ. In 2 Corinthians 5:19–20, Paul says: "To wit, that God was in Christ, reconciling the world unto himself, not imputing their trespasses unto them; and hath committed unto us the word of reconciliation. Now then we are ambassadors for Christ, as though God did beseech you by us: we pray you in Christ's stead, be ye reconciled to God."

The best investments for eternity are those we have led to the Lord. Carry good Gospel tracts and church brochures as well as a New Testament. Be ready to talk to others about the Lord, or to hand out a Gospel tract. First Peter 3:15 says, "But sanctify the Lord God in your hearts: and be ready always to give an answer to every man that asketh you a reason of the hope that is in you with meekness and fear." Imagine spending eternity without seeing even one individual that you witnessed to. Conversely, think of the great joy of meeting those in Heaven whom you have helped to win.

Finances you have given

As God has provided for our needs, we are to honor Him. Proverbs 3:9 says, "Honour the LORD with thy substance, and with the firstfruits of all thine increase." As we give to the Lord through our local church, we lay up an investment in eternity. Matthew 6:20 says, "But lay up for yourselves treasures in heaven, where neither moth nor rust doth corrupt, and where thieves do not break through nor steal."

The opportunities are immense in the Lord's work, and we must joyfully give to the Lord in tithes and offerings, because they are really God's, and they are an eternal investment. God help us to live and invest wisely for eternity.

The Rapture We Will Experience

Careful Bible study indicates that the Rapture or catching away of the church is rapidly approaching—it could happen today. It is imminent—nothing else has to happen first.

Little Johnny delighted to hear and count the chiming of the hours by the large grandfather clock in the living room. At noon one day, he lay on the floor counting each gong as it sounded. This day something went wrong with the clock's mechanism. Instead of stopping at twelve gongs, it kept chiming. Johnny jumped to his feet and ran to the kitchen shouting, "Mommy, Mommy, it's later than it's ever been before."

Today is later than it has ever been before. Romans 13:11 states, "And that, knowing the time, that now it is high time to awake out of sleep: for now is our salvation nearer than when we believed." And James 5:8 says, "Be ye also patient; stablish your hearts: for the coming of the Lord draweth nigh." Men have tried repeatedly to establish a fixed time that Christ will return. They've never been right because Jesus said that no one but the Father knows the day or hour, but we know our Lord's coming is soon. Titus 2:13 says, "Looking for that blessed hope, and the glorious appearing of the great God and our Saviour Jesus Christ."

A sudden event

The Rapture is described in the Bible as sudden and unannounced. First Corinthians 15:51–52 says, "Behold, I shew you a mystery; We shall not all sleep, but we shall all be changed, In a moment, in the twinkling of an eye, at the last trump: for the trumpet shall sound, and the dead shall be raised incorruptible, and we shall be changed." First Thessalonians 4:16 says, "For the Lord himself shall descend from heaven with a shout, with the voice of the archangel, and with the trump of God: and the dead in Christ shall rise first."

Just that quickly, we will hear a shout with the voice of the archangel, the trumpet will sound, and we will be gone! Notice, we leave "in a moment." In Greek, *atomos*, our English word is *atom*, a small particle or a twinkling of an eye. General Electric says the twinkling lasts about 11/100 of a second. This unannounced, instantaneous event could be today so, "watch and be sober."

A selective event

The Rapture is reserved for all of the saved ones in this Church Age—both those who have died in Christ and those who are alive at His return. First Thessalonians 4:14–15 says, "For if we believe that

Jesus died and rose again, even so them also which sleep in Jesus will God bring with him. For this we say unto you by the word of the Lord, that we which are alive and remain unto the coming of the Lord shall not prevent them which are asleep."

Only the redeemed are a part of this wonderful event, and there will be no opportunity or chance for anyone to make a last-minute decision. All the lost will remain on the earth to suffer and go through the Great Tribulation. The Old Testament and Tribulation saints will have their resurrection at the end of the Tribulation.

A surprising event

What a surprise and joy to meet those who refused the Gospel when you witnessed to them only to find that they had received Christ later. By your faithful soulwinning efforts, the seed was sown. Remember Paul's words in 1 Corinthians 3:6–7, "I have planted, Apollos watered; but God gave the increase. So then neither is he that planteth any thing, neither he that watereth; but God that giveth the increase."

Others that you were sure would be present will be absent because they were only professing Christians, and were never really saved. Matthew 7:22–23, "Many will say to me in that day, Lord, Lord, have we not prophesied in thy name? and in thy name have cast out devils? and in thy name done many wonderful works? And then will I profess unto them, I never knew you: depart from me, ye that work iniquity." It will be absolutely shocking to see who is present and who is left behind when we get to Heaven.

A sobering event

All of our earthly labors will be over and we will not be able to do any more of the Lord's work. Paul says in 1 Corinthians 15:58, "Therefore, my beloved brethren, be ye stedfast, unmoveable, always abounding in the work of the Lord, forasmuch as ye know that your labour is not in vain in the Lord." We are told to be "steadfast" in our faith and in doctrinal truth. Then we should be "unmoveable" in our daily living as we walk through this wicked world. First John 3:3 says, "And every man that hath this hope in him purifieth himself, even as he is pure." The Christian man must "always be abounding" wherever God has placed him. Don't quit or cave in, but be always busy about the Father's business.

Our labor is never purposeless, although we may be exhausted and unaware of its ultimate purpose. God blesses and honors our faithful service, so don't drop by the wayside as you minister. Galatians 6:9 says, "And let us not be weary in well doing: for in due season we shall reap, if we faint not." We must live wisely and soberly because eternity waits.

The Rewards We Will Receive

The first experience we will have after the Rapture is the Judgment Seat of Christ. Second Corinthians 5:10 says, "For we must all appear before the judgment seat of Christ; that every one may receive the things done in his body, according to that he hath done, whether it be good or bad."

The Bema Judgment will reveal much about us because He knows all things—our thoughts and motives as well as our actions. First Corinthians 3:13–16 says, "Every man's work shall be made manifest: for the day shall declare it, because it shall be revealed by fire; and the fire shall try every man's work of what sort it is. If any man's work abide which he hath built thereupon, he shall receive a reward. If any man's work shall be burned, he shall suffer loss: but he himself shall be saved; yet so as by fire. Know ye not that ye are the temple of God, and that the Spirit of God dwelleth in you?"

Think of what will be burned because we tried to build our lives with wood, hay, and stubble. All of the empty things or service with wrong motive will not last the test before our Master. However, every service truly done for the Lord anywhere will not go unnoticed, even a cup of water given in Christ's name will not lose a reward. Revelation 22:12 says, "And, behold, I come quickly; and my reward is with me, to give every man according as his work shall be." I trust you will not lose rewards, but secure them. Revelation 3:11 says, "Behold, I come quickly: hold that fast which thou hast, that no man take thy crown."

Remember, we will be individually and justly rewarded by Christ. First Corinthians 3:8 says, "Now he that planteth and he that watereth are one: and every man shall receive his own reward according to his own labour." The Word of God speaks about several different crowns awaiting us at the Judgment Seat of Christ. Are any of these crowns awaiting you at His coming?

The Incorruptible Crown

First Corinthians 9:25, "And every man that striveth for the mastery is temperate in all things. Now they do it to obtain a corruptible crown; but we an incorruptible." Here Paul uses the analogy of a runner in a race who follows the rules as he keeps himself under control.

We know that our flesh wants to sin and disobey God, but we must allow the Holy Spirit to control us. Ephesians 5:18 says, "And be not drunk with wine, wherein is excess; but be filled with the Spirit." If we are surrendered to the indwelling Holy Spirit, we can live godly before the Lord. Galatians 5:16 says, "This I say then, Walk in the Spirit, and ye shall not fulfil the lust of the flesh."

Paul states that he tried to walk carefully so that he would not run outside the rules and find himself disqualified from receiving the Incorruptible Crown. First Corinthians 9:27, "But I keep under my body, and bring it into subjection: lest that by any means, when I have preached to others, I myself should be a castaway."

The Crown of Rejoicing

Paul's ongoing passion was to reach the lost with the Gospel, and everywhere Paul traveled, he left a trail of converts. Paul was bold to preach the Gospel everywhere. Now he speaks of a special crown awaiting him because of the souls saved through his work. First Thessalonians 2:19 says, "For what is our hope, or joy, or crown of rejoicing? Are not even ye in the presence of our Lord Jesus Christ at his coming?"

Paul needed God's boldness in preaching the Gospel, and so do we. Ephesians 6:19–20 says, "And for me, that utterance may be given unto me, that I may open my mouth boldly, to make known the mystery of the gospel, For which I am an ambassador in bonds: that therein I may speak boldly, as I ought to speak."

The Crown of Righteousness

Paul is on the final leg of his life, awaiting execution from the Roman government. He summarizes his life and ministry in 2 Timothy 4:7, "I have fought a good fight, I have finished my course, I have kept the faith."

As Paul looks back, he gives a clear statement of his commitment to Christ. He speaks of a special crown that he anticipates will be presented to him by his Saviour. In 2 Timothy 4:8 he says, "Henceforth there is laid up for me a crown of righteousness, which the Lord, the righteous judge, shall give me at that day: and not to me only, but unto all them also that love his appearing."

Are you looking for Christ's return? It will motivate you, purify you, propel you, and reward you with a special reward called the Crown of Righteousness.

The Crown of Life

According to James, the Crown of Life is reserved for the child of God who endures the trials and temptations of life. All of us will have hardships and trials. The common saying "into every life some rain must fall" is very true. These trials can seem overwhelming; Satan uses these to try to defeat us. However, we have One with us who has promised to never leave us or forsake us, and who is ready to come to our aid and succour us. Hebrews 2:18 states, "For in that he himself hath suffered being tempted, he is able to succour them that are tempted."

We also face the temptations of the world, the flesh and the devil, as these three enemies of the soul march against us. Drawn away by our fleshly desires, we are tempted to yield to sin. James 1:14–15, "But every man is tempted, when he is drawn away of his own lust, and enticed. Then when lust hath conceived, it bringeth forth sin: and sin, when it is finished, bringeth forth death." But we are equipped by the indwelling Holy Spirit, the Word of God, and all the resources of Heaven so that we can win. The Saviour will present the Crown of Life to those He thinks are worthy of it. Will you receive this crown?

The Crown of Glory

The Crown of Glory will be presented to the faithful undershepherd by the chief shepherd, the Lord Jesus. The man who unashamedly proclaims the Word of God will be presented this crown. A faithful pastor and teacher of the Scriptures leads his flock and feeds his flock to nourish them and make them useful for Christ. Ephesians 4:12–13 says, "For the perfecting of the saints, for the work of the ministry, for the edifying of the body of Christ: Till we all come in the unity of the faith, and of the knowledge of the Son of God, unto a perfect man, unto the measure of the stature of the fullness of Christ."

This special crown is well deserved to godly, faithful men as Peter states in 1 Peter 5:2–4, "Feed the flock of God which is among you, taking the oversight thereof, not by constraint, but willingly; not for filthy lucre, but of a ready mind; Neither as being lords over God's heritage, but being ensamples to the flock. And when the chief Shepherd shall appear, ye shall receive a crown of glory that fadeth not away." Love, support, and encourage your pastor as he labors in the Word and faithfully leads the flock in your local church, and share in the blessing of seeing him receive this Crown of Glory.

The Crown of Life

Now we have already mentioned the Crown of Life found in James 1:12, but now we find this reward mentioned again, this time in Revelation 2:10, "Fear none of those things which thou shalt suffer: behold, the devil shall cast some of you into prison, that ye may be tried; and ye shall have tribulation ten days: be thou faithful unto death, and I will give thee a crown of life."

Revelation speaks of a crown for those believers that face death for the love of their Saviour. Myriads of Christians have faced a martyr's death. The courage of God's people is a testimony to the grace of God. Today, faithful believers around the world are being tortured and killed for their testimony. Hebrews 11 says of the persecuted, faithful, and martyrs through the ages, "(Of whom the world was not worthy)…." At the Judgment Seat, many of us will have to take a back seat as we watch the parade of those martyrs who died for their faith. What honor will be bestowed on these as they receive the Crown of Life!

All the rewards and crowns in Revelation have now been presented. Revelation 4:10–11 says, "The four and twenty elders fall down before him that sat on the throne, and worship him that liveth for ever and ever, and cast their crowns before the throne, saying, Thou art worthy, O Lord, to receive glory and honour and power: for thou hast created all things, and for thy pleasure they are and were created."

I cannot understand the meeting with my Saviour when He will reward me with what He decides is right. With tears of joy and gratitude I will lay those rewards and crowns before my Sovereign King. What about you? What will you have to present to your Saviour?

Reigning with Christ

The Judgment Seat of Christ is past, the Marriage Supper of the Lamb has concluded, and we return to earth with our King, the Saviour, for the Battle of Armageddon—Revelation 19:11–15: "And I saw heaven opened, and behold a white horse; and he that sat upon him was called Faithful and True, and in righteousness he doth judge and make war. His eyes were as a flame of fire, and on his head were many crowns; and he had a name written, that no man knew, but he himself. And he was clothed with a vesture dipped in blood: and his name is called The Word of God. And the armies which were in heaven followed him upon white horses, clothed in fine linen, white and clean. And out of his mouth goeth a sharp sword, that with it he should smite the nations: and he shall rule them with a rod of iron: and he treadeth the winepress of the fierceness and wrath of Almighty God."

In this battle in the Valley of Jezreel, the enemies of God, Satan, and the false prophet are defeated. Revelation 19:20 says, "And the beast was taken, and with him the false prophet that wrought miracles before him, with which he deceived them that had received the mark of the beast, and them that worshipped his image...."

Other things happen, but the most important event is the inauguration of the long prophesied rule of Christ as King of kings begins. This thousand year period, which we call the Millennium, will be like no other time on earth because the rightful King rules, and Satan is bound in the bottomless pit for that thousand years.

We get to reign with Christ. Revelation 5:10 says, "And hast made us unto our God kings and priests: and we shall reign on the earth." While we do not know the details of our reign with Him, we will reign with Him as He sits on David's throne. The Scriptures seem to indicate the measure of our ruling with Christ will be in relation to our rewards from Him.

Following the thousand years, Satan will be loosed for a season, then finally thrown in the lake of fire and eternity will begin. We will worship, praise, and serve Him forever. John concludes the Word of God with these precious verses. Revelation 22:20–21, "He which testifieth these things saith, Surely I come quickly. Amen. Even so, come, Lord Jesus. The grace of our Lord Jesus Christ be with you all. Amen."

SUMMARY OF THIS CHAPTER

As we reflect on the soon return of Christ, then facing His judgment of our work, we are sobered. I hope you live always thinking that today might be the day He returns.

I. The Realities We Live
II. The Rapture We Will Experience
III. The Rewards We Will Receive
IV. Reigning with Christ

ACTION STEPS

Here are three action steps you can take as you consider the return of Christ and the results of your life. (Initial and date when completed.)

1. List on a sheet of paper and reflect on the areas you have wisely invested in as you face eternity.

   Initial _____ Date _____

2. As you have read through the "Six Crowns" list, can you think of which one or ones you might receive at the Judgment Seat of Christ? List these on a 3x5 card and determine to see the list grow.

   Initial _____ Date _____

3. When you arrive in Heaven will there be others to greet you and thank you for your soulwinning efforts? Maybe you could even list a few names.

   Initial _____ Date _____

CONCLUSION
by Martha Martens

Almost forty-five years ago I witnessed the beginning of my husband taking steps to become a man of God. There was the initial step of surrendering his will to the will of God. Then he started developing a walk with God by spending diligent time in God's Word, faithful attendance to God's house and then consecration to serve God!

Over the past forty-four years I have seen God develop "my honey" into an incredible, godly man. He had a sterling work ethic (any job worth doing should be done right). He learned early on that there would be battles—both fleshly and spiritual—and that the only way to have victory was by "putting on the whole armour of God." His resolve to face trials and temptations by turning to God and His Word brought victory over and through trials and developed a confidence in the *truth* of the Word that never wavered. Wherever he preached, he would hold up the Bible and challenge the listener to know the Word, believe the Word, and then *live* the

Word. Whether he was preaching to a group or talking one-on-one to someone, he would first pray for the Holy Spirit's guidance, and then he would predicate everything he said based on the Word of God.

Over the years, God used him to be a friend to many, many men—young and old alike—and during the weeks following his home-going, so many men called or wrote notes to tell me how he had been "a best friend" to them. One of the things they would mention was that "he was real" and didn't "put on airs." And he enjoyed *life*! We had the philosophy that we were going to "live each day to the fullest," and because of that, God used him to be an encouragement to those he came in contact with along the way.

God blessed him with a fruitful ministry of seeing souls saved and grounded in the Word, and then many going on to serve the Lord—both as lay servants and full-time servants. And up until the hour God took him Home, he was meditating on Scripture— asking for God's direction on what to preach the following Sunday. His life (our life) was full and overflowing with God's blessings. Was he rich? Materially—no; but in eternal riches—yes! With riches that will never fade away. In fact, he's enjoying many of those riches right now!

While he was on this earth he (we) had learned that the greatest riches were to see our "children walk in truth" and to walk in obedience to God's Word daily ourselves. He would often quote "Trust and obey, for there's no other way to be happy in Jesus, but to trust and obey." And then he would say, "living the Christian life is simple—the hard part is dying to self."

We had a great family life rearing our children; we had a great life together as husband and wife; and we had a blessed life serving our Saviour—together!

Looking back over the last several years of his life, I can sum it up with two thoughts:

1. **No Regrets—because he lived each day with purpose: to glorify his Saviour.**

2. **He walked with God and "was no more."**

The key to this awesome life is that he "kept looking unto Jesus…" and was faithful to God, his wife and his family. What a "ride" we had!

The best is yet to come for those of us here on this earth. "My honey" would challenge each of us to live life in light of eternity—not for the "here and now." And he would tell us to invest our time and our lives in people—because they live forever and ever and ever. Do what you can to make a difference in someone else's life that will last for eternity! Share the Gospel. Take time to disciple new believers. Be an encourager of fellow-believers!

Oh Christian, live life to the fullest—for our Saviour. God tells us in John 10:10b, "I am come that they might have life, and that they might have it more abundantly."

By His wonderful grace,
Martha Martens

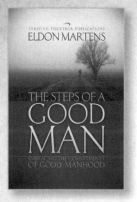
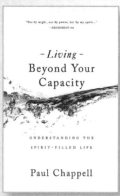
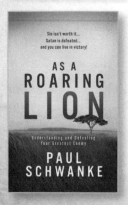

Visit us online

strivingtogether.com

wcbc.edu